The Experiential Approach

Copyright © 2012 by Dean Nelson

All rights reserved. No part of this book may be reproduced by any mechanical, photographic, or electronic process, or in the form of an audio recording of any kind. This book may not be stored in a retrieval system, transmitted, or otherwise copied for public or private use other than using brief quotations embodied in articles or reviews, without prior written permission of the publisher.

The author of this book does not dispense medical advice or prescribe the use of any technique or exercise in this book as a form of treatment for physical, mental, emotional or medical problems without the advice of a physician, either directly or indirectly. The author intends only to offer general information that may assist in your quest for spiritual, emotional or physical well-being. Should you use any information in this book for yourself, which is your constitutional right, the author and the publisher assume no responsibility for your results or your actions.

Copyright © 2012 by Dean Nelson

ISBN 978-0-9914558-0-5

Seven Cardinal Gates
Publishing

The Experiential Approach

A Fresh New Approach

For Creating Immediate

Personal Power

Dean Nelson

Seven Cardinal Gates
Publishing

Acknowledgements

Dedicated to my best friend and loving wife of more than 33 years, Paula. You taught me so much about life and helped me become a better husband, father and person. Thank you for your patience, love and understanding. May we experience peace, love and fulfillment in all of our time together.

My deepest appreciation and love to all those who have inspired and supported me throughout this endeavor.

Thank you Tina Peak for your kind-hearted, honest approach and your tireless hours of work editing and advising me throughout this entire process. I am immensely blessed and grateful for your friendship.

I am also extremely grateful to my family; Paula, my brother

Van and his wife Bonnie; my daughters, Jenna and Jaclyn; my mother and stepfather, Alice and Richard Stark for your input, love and undying support.

Great appreciation is also felt for Steve and Georgianna Sorensen, Marla and Tony Barone, and Tim and Sue Raible for your invaluable advice, positive influence, gratifying support and wonderful friendship throughout the years.

Special thanks to Becky Rupp for your encouragement from the outset with only the first two chapters written. Also, to Marie Zero for your much appreciated assistance in a pinch.

May the Divine infuse your lives with peace, love, perfect harmony and well-being.

When a notion is converted into a belief, the creative power of the Universe is unleashed and the manifestation of a miracle is at hand.

— Dean Nelson

Contents

Chapter One

A Shotgun In The Shower 9

Chapter Two

What It Is And Why It Works 23

Chapter Three

What Are Beliefs And How Do They Affect Our Lives? 49

Chapter Four

Are Your Intentions Powerful? 77

Chapter Five

Exactly How Important Are The Choices We Make? 105

Chapter Six

Actions Speak Louder Than Words 125

Chapter Seven

Tying It All Together And Making It Happen 155

About The Author 175

Recommended Resources 177

Chapter One

A Shotgun In The Shower

My life changed forever one tragic September afternoon in 1972. Virtually witnessing my father's suicide that Sunday and the guilt I experienced haunted me for decades.

I was a typically rebellious fifteen year old anticipating my first year in a small high school. It is in the nature of adolescents to push away from their parents, and then pull them back in again. I was playing this push and pull game with my father. My long hair, my friends and my attitude were wearing on our relationship.

I was also aware that my mother and father were having problems of their own.

I did not realize how deep their marital problems had grown until the afternoon my overwrought mother told me my dad had placed a 12-gauge shotgun in their shower.

She was terrified and confused. She needed help, but she did not want to involve our neighbors.

I had to call for help.

My parents had trusted friends. I knew I could call them, but the closest public pay phone was a half-mile away. Understanding the desperate situation our family was in I ran. When I reached the pay phone I dropped my only coin in and dialed.

I heard a voice answer on the other end and immediately knew that I misdialed.

The voice on the line answered from our local police department.

I hesitated when the dispatcher answered. Did I want to risk the police being dispatched to our home? My teenage mind quickly reasoned that I didn't know what my father's intentions were, but I knew that he had a volatile temper.

I quickly told the police dispatcher I'd dialed the wrong number and placed the receiver back on its cradle. How I could have possibly known that number or just coincidentally misdialed it remains a mystery.

I ran to a nearby gas station and asked to use their phone to report an emergency.

As I reached my parents' friends I quickly told Delores there was an emergency. She dropped everything and arrived at our home before I returned on foot.

Despite my mom's desire not to involve the neighbors, our next door neighbor was in our yard. When I explained the frightening situation unfolding in our house he offered to enter with me.

There was an eerie stillness and a deafening silence in our small home. As I approached my parents' bedroom I began to call out to my father, "Dad, Dad!" There was no reply.

I tried to open the door, it was locked. In that instant a shotgun blast broke the silence. My mind was racing with panic and fear. Our concerned neighbor had run for safety along with my mom and Delores who, unbeknownst to me, were hiding in our utility room.

They left me alone and scared with the unknown.

I did not try to unlock the bedroom door, but ran outside to their bathroom window. I again called to my father, "Dad.

Dad!"

I had no other words, no appeals for rational conversation, and no heartfelt pleas for him to come out and talk to us. I stood there, terrified and mute after calling to him twice.

My 15-year-old self returned inside, feeling alone in this waking nightmare that was unfolding in my own home. I began walking to his bedroom, calling to him one more time, "Dad." That cry to my father was answered with a muffled blast. This time I reached for a hidden key and with trembling hands I opened the locked bedroom door.

A heavy fog of smoke hung in layers across the still room. The smell of spent gunpowder was overpowering. I noticed a large hole in the dresser, but I did not see my father.

I was alone in the room; trembling violently.

I knew what I had to do and willed my youthful self toward the open bathroom door.

The horror of my father's lifeless body, the sound of his blood oozing from the wound and trickling down the drain was something that haunted me for many years. In that instant I experienced the deep, visceral pain of loss and despair. I ran from the home I'd shared with my family, met by the sirens of police and ambulance, the growing crowd of concerned neighbors and my mother's deep grief.

I was the first to know, our father was gone.

The Dark Side

The twenty years following that September afternoon were the darkest of my life. Slipping in and out of depression and suicidal thoughts of my own; I lived with tormenting guilt and shame for what I perceived as my inadequate actions on the day my father died.

This is my first attempt at putting this very personal story on paper; speaking it out loud. I have shared this tragedy with only selected family members and a few trusted instructors; teachers who worked with me during life-transforming Avatar seminars I attended in the years since then. Avatar is a powerful self-development program with many insightful experiential exercises.

I share this graphic and painful story simply in hope that you will comprehend the incredible pain and anguish I experienced at a very young age.

I want you, the reader to understand that the most devastating experience, an unthinkable memory, can be accepted and overcome. Our darkest recollections can be transformed, neutralized and rendered powerless in their effects on our lives.

My story will lead through simple ways to make lasting change in your life, no matter what darkness your life's story includes.

Facing many challenges and harmful beliefs, my journey to recovery was long and characterized by periods of excess grief and stress.

I was deeply affected by my father's suicide letter to our family. The letter declared his love for our family, but his belief that he was a failure as a husband and a father.

My father's final letter and my belief that my actions on the day of his death contributed to his suicide affected me for decades.

I held to the beliefs that my father's suicide was because I was a rebellious teenager, I wasn't the ideal son he wanted and that I had missed opportunities to save him on that

September afternoon.

Why hadn't I asked for assistance from the police when I misdialed? Why didn't I plead with my father when I had the chance? Why had I wasted time running a half-mile to call for help when any of our neighbors would have allowed me to call for help from their phones?

My self-doubt evolved into a list of destructive beliefs. I believed that I was unworthy, doomed to fail. I believed that my deepest failure was to my father, my family, my God and myself.

Seek and Ye Shall Find

At age twenty-five I began a search for ways to break free from the bondage of self-doubt and destruction.

A friend recommended an audio program by Dr. Dennis Waitley, *The Psychology of Winning,* (Nightingale-Conant). Listening to Dr. Waitley's inspirational and educational program gave me insight and encouragement.

My personal quest for self-improvement and enlightenment

had begun.

Over the course of twenty years I spent $20,000 investing in books, recordings, films and seminars. Learning about positive thinking and self-talk, meditation and stress reduction, affirmations, goal setting, power of beliefs and choices, and so much more were avenues of interest that I pursued with vigor.

Even after my huge expenditure the self-doubt was still at the core of my being. I had done a masterful job of resisting, denying and pushing these beliefs back; so masterful, in fact, that I no longer realized they remained.

But they were still there, guiding my every move, sabotaging and setting the pace for my life and controlling my destiny.

Throughout the emotional ordeal and aftermath of my father's suicide I continued to have a close bond with my mom and my brother, Van.

Van remains a positive influence and role model. His courage and discipline following Dad's death was amazing. At the young age of 19 he handled difficult family situations with the maturity of a much older adult. My life might have taken a darker path without his love and involvement.

In spite of this I resisted some of Van's advice and assistance to pursue my own avenues of interest. I held no ill feelings toward Van, but there were undercurrents of jealousy over what I perceived as his *easy life.*

During this period of my life it was as if I was determined to fail, but had something to prove. I wanted to be left alone, make my own mistakes and find my own way out of the fog.

My wife, Paula, tried for years to break me out of my self-centered world. Paula was patient, open-minded, forgiving and supportive. She provided a warm, loving environment; nurturing our family and raising our two incredibly wonderful daughters, Jenna and Jaclyn.

Paula was instrumental in the regression of my painful, stress-induced, Ulcerative Colitis by providing a book authored by Jon Kabat-Zinn, *Full Catastrophe Living: Using the Wisdom of Your Body and Mind to Face Stress,*

Pain and Illness.

Her help was a major turning point in my life resulting in a delightful change from the miserable physical state I had unwittingly placed myself in.

Even with strong and loving family support my good intentions were held in check due to my negative beliefs.

I floundered for years, making poor choices and wondering why life seemed difficult for me.

At age 45 I attended an Avatar seminar. My life was catapulted into an exciting and fulfilling path. Thirty years after my father's suicide I finally chased down the beliefs that gripped me. I experienced these beliefs and, with great emotional release, allowed them to vanish.

I accepted that there is no power in the universe greater than the power of belief.

I also realized there is no action, event, situation, experience, condition or thought that does not involve or relate to our beliefs, intentions or choices.

Everything we think, do and say is controlled by and

filtered through our beliefs, intentions and choices.

Belief begets and fuels the power of intention. Intention propels us forward and ultimately the power of choice determines our destiny by selecting paths for our lives and opening doors to our future.

The knowledge I gained from Avatar seminars opened doors for creating a new belief system. It introduced me to an exciting life of contentment and bliss.

The following chapters will guide you through a simple formula to empower yourself to achieve your greatest potential; with marked results in a few days.

I am grateful for the opportunity to share with those seeking assistance in these areas of their lives.

I have been blessed by my wife, my family and the many authors, teachers and instructors who have helped me on this life-changing journey.

My hope is this book will provide a much shorter path to you than the one I chose.

I believe it is my calling and destiny to share this important information with many who are seeking a more fulfilled life.

My intention is to assist those desiring transformation or improvement in their current situation.

May your journey be meaningful and blessed.

Chapter Two

What It Is and Why It Works

The road I traveled from the darkest and most devastating event to my present happiness and peace was not a straight or direct one.

For over 20 years I sought answers from self-help books, tapes, films and seminars. As the result of my years of research I am convinced I have found a very effective and simple method to implement behavioral, emotional and attitudinal improvements with rapid results.

What I will share is a method that saved me and showed me how to find and accept peace in my life.

You will gain powerful insights from the short and enjoyable exercises found in this book.

The tools I developed through the instruction I experienced in the Avatar seminars had the greatest effect on my life.

The process I have developed in this book evolved from a

combination of Avatar System tools and other resources.

We all have personal preferences and traits. Our nature as humans draws us to a variety of music, food, religious beliefs, leisure activities and careers. We are defined by our individual traits and preferences.

Many self-help books and programs offer helpful advice and reliable techniques. Each serves a purpose and shares information that appeals to a variety of personalities.

It is my belief the methods I teach in this book will work for anyone who follows the steps and implements the simple and powerful techniques.

I will explore with you a variety of principles and techniques that meld together a variety of teachings and philosophies.

Each individual seeking a new path will find a smorgasbord of philosophies. It is my hope that by sharing what led me down the path to inner peace you can find a similar path in the tools I used.

After the devastation I experienced I looked for answers in seminars and books. I sought the best options for improving the quality of my life.

I input the phrase "self-improvement seminars" in an internet search engine. There were over 549,000 results returned! Then I tried "self-improvement books" and I received 5.5 million results! Next I entered "self-help books" which revealed a whopping 122,000,000 results!

Obviously, millions of people have the desire to make needed changes. Many have not found a system or approach that provides comfort and confidence needed for success. If there was a "one size fits all" approach the previous statistics would be very different.

The person who wants or needs to make changes in their life may or may not find success with this book, but the one who is *ready* to make these changes will surely be successful.

Years ago my wife and I lived near a Florida nature preserve. We took night walks bringing along a spotlight. We directed the bright beam on a variety of wildlife including owls, raccoons, armadillos and wild boar.

The light gave us an opportunity to observe these creatures, noticing details we would have missed without the bright spotlight.

Use this book to shine a spotlight on your life. Looking closely at fresh ideas with new tools will help effect life change in a positive, straightforward manner.

Procrastination Fascination

Are you often late for work or other engagements? Do you avoid paying bills, attending family events or completing assigned tasks? Do you forget to return phone calls, complete chores or follow up with clients?

It is believed that twenty percent of adults in America are chronic procrastinators. Procrastination can be debilitating and may ultimately derail personal success.

Procrastination can lead to troubled relationships, personal credit issues, job instability, frustration and stress that can ultimately affect personal health and happiness.

Individuals who struggle with procrastination may feel compelled to avoid or delay even the simplest activities or decisions.

Creating To-Do lists, writing notes or using a day planner are essential tools for a procrastinator, but these tools don't address the core issues of this behavior.

The processes that will be addressed in this book will reveal underlying causes of procrastination and provide avenues for overcoming these energy zapping hang-ups in a rapid, effective manner.

Are you ready to set aside inaction and move ahead to greater success and accomplish more of your goals?

It's the Little Things That Matter

At one point in my life I began to lose patience with myself. Many daily routines were becoming frustrating and stressful.

One major trigger of daily frustration was a software program utilized by my company, Customer Relationship Management tool, or CRM.

One frustrating element of this program was the email

feature, which had a programming glitch.

Email was my primary form of communication with customers, co-workers and staff.

My frustration with CRM focused on the program's irritating habit of jumping the cursor up a row as I entered text. At times I looked up from my paperwork to the monitor and realized words I'd intended for one sentence were now inserted in the row above.

I had several choice words for the software provider with each frequent occurrence.

This may seem trite to you but as I experienced it on a day after day basis I felt that the software glitch resulted in a common stressor. It was an easy target for utilizing the process explained in my book.

Having experienced enough frustration, I realized that I had the tools to bring this situation under control. I chose to use the valuable technique I'd mastered along the way.

The results were quick and effective. My daily attitude improved immediately.

You'll soon be introduced to this effective technique in the pages of my book.

Prescription Please!

I discovered that I had transparent, or hidden, beliefs that were the basis of my frustration. I use the term *transparent* because the beliefs were hidden to me. I did not realize that I was carrying them with me in my belief bank.

The owner of the business I was employed at had once stated, "Men lose patience as they age."

He explained that he was experiencing more frustration with situations and he had less patience with each passing year.

I agreed with him and adopted his belief that *men lose patience as they age.* I felt I was losing patience as I grew older.

I found other transparent beliefs that I harbored. These disempowering beliefs included; 'I don't have the patience I used to have,' ' I am more impatient with myself than I am with others,' (my wife may disagree with that one).

Hidden beliefs were interfering with my day to day business and personal life.

The simple remedy was the creation of new beliefs and powerful intentions that would carry my life forward in a positive direction.

The magical element of the process included the magnification of choices presented in the following days.

As I decided to implement change in my life, a powerful intention, the normal choices that I previously ignored were still there, however they were now magnified as a flashing neon light as each opportunity became available.

This was a result of releasing my old beliefs, creating new beliefs and powerful intentions and watching as the neon lights shown.

As old beliefs were released and replaced with new positive beliefs there was a shift in my thinking. It was not until I created the powerful intentions that I felt a significant event was on the horizon.

Each time I felt myself in the grasp of a stressful episode the choice was clear; allow the stress to consume me or face the situation head on and choose not to let it bother me. The two were like red and green blinking lights beckoning me to choose one or the other.

The obvious choice was avoid the stress. Anticipating the next opportunity to make another choice became exciting. Over and over again each day opportunities for choices presented themselves.

My new beliefs and powerful intentions were leading me to a new attitude for life.

By the end of week one I was, quite literally, chuckling at what I used to consider stressors. I found myself keenly aware of other work related stressors as well.

It was easy for me to decide not to harbor these stressors. At first I experienced the stress instantly, and then chose to let it go. As each stressful situation arose it became easier to make the choice to avoid the stress.

Making the Right Choices

The key to success in life, and with this program, is making the right choices. Nothing else we do will matter if our choices are constantly wrong. Of course, we all make erroneous choices but if our beliefs are sound and our intentions powerful, choices will present themselves that give rise to opportunity for success.

The more conviction we hold in our beliefs and the more power we transmit to our intentions, the more immense and abundant are the choices and the opportunities for happy and successful lives.

The option to succeed or fail is always there for each of us. We have the propensity for walking in the dark or following the light based on our daily choices.

TMI

Too Much Information can overload our system and cause stress in our lives. My book is short and to the point for this very reason.

One reason people have difficulties determining and achieving goals is they *may* have created too many goals to realistically achieve in a limited time frame.

Humans have limited attention capacity. When this attention span is taxed we stress, when we bear too much stress we ultimately function at an impoverished level.

This book teaches simple and effective means of creating space for goals, or intentions, that you will implement immediately. The results will be quickly evident, motivating you to create more powerful intentions.

A *goal* is a wish or dream, a desire or a purpose you wish to attain for your life.

A *powerful intention* is a *goal* that has been optimized; purged of transparent beliefs. A powerful intention incorporates a powerful new belief and the emotional feelings attached to it.

My process will give rise to steady, positive and rapid results moving you forward. The results are exciting and rewarding.

Discovering Transparent Beliefs

The first step in creating new beliefs and powerful intentions is to discover your *transparent beliefs*; beliefs held within your subconscious mind that you are unaware of.

You don't realize these beliefs are there because they are just below the surface, transparent and hidden from you. But they are at work all the time, guiding your decisions, influencing every move you make.

Transparent beliefs will effectively guide us through life. Discovering what transparent beliefs we hold is important. They may hinder or help our progress. Eliminating these negative beliefs and replacing them with positive, empowering beliefs will support our navigation through life.

Beliefs can be like banana trees. We recently transplanted several banana trees located near our herb garden. They were blocking the sun the herbs thrive on. The trees we moved into our outdoor shower area were the result of one banana tree we originally planted. The multiple trees were offshoots of the single tree and each new tree was producing its own shoots.

Beliefs may attach to a core belief and begin to cluster and sprout other beliefs.

The example I provided earlier, "men lose patience as they age," sprouted the additional beliefs, "I don't have the patience I used to have," and "I am more impatient with my own shortcomings than I am with others."

While deeply exploring a single belief you hold, hidden beliefs that are lurking in the shadows will be revealed.

The following exercise is adapted from *Resurfacing: Techniques for Exploring Consciousness,* a book by Harry Palmer, creator of the Avatar materials. The simple exercise will bring to light transparent, hidden beliefs that may be interfering with your attainment of goals.

To begin the exercise, locate a quiet place where you can concentrate, undisturbed, for fifteen minutes. During the process you may discover hidden beliefs in a few moments, or it may be a slower process. Each individual has a unique experience. Take your time, relax and enjoy the process. This exercise is fun and quite rewarding, especially when a hidden belief reveals itself.

During a four year period I spent over 400 hours in Avatar classroom settings. I learned many techniques, practicing them alone and with countless others.

I have not only experienced incredible personal insights and gains but I have witnessed hundreds of people from the far reaches of the globe experience enlightening transformations.

I believe that if you don't have goals and powerful intentions for your life, you're missing excitement in your life. As your transparent belief is revealed you will have the most important piece of information to assist you in creating new beliefs and powerful intentions.

Exercise 1

Discovering Transparent Beliefs

Ideally this exercise is performed with an assistant. The assistant reads the steps aloud and coaches you through the process. The exercise can be done alone, but if you attempt it by yourself and the results are not what you hoped for, finding a willing assistant that you can trust may have satisfying results.

Please be honest and respond to the questions with answers that come to mind.

If your answers seem undeniably true you may discover something interesting. Your proof for owning that belief is probably the proof being produced by that belief. You are not creating the proof; your *belief* is creating the proof. Your belief is your reality.

You will need two sheets of paper and a pen to begin the exercise. The first sheet of paper is for the transparent belief exercise. You will save this sheet and retrieve it later when you're ready to complete the entire process.

Step One – Draw a vertical line down the center of the paper. At the top of the Left column write *Issues*, and at the top of the Right column write *Old Beliefs*.

Step Two – Determine what you want to change in your life. If you are working with an assistant they should pose the question, "What would you like to change in your life?" If no assistant, ask the question aloud to yourself. The question should be repeated until a situation or thought is revealed. Answer the question aloud. The answer should be recorded under the *Issues* column by you or your assistant.

Step Two identifies the change you would like to happen in your life. The questions in Step Three reveal the beliefs that are creating the situation preventing the desired change. The questions also pinpoint the experiences that are reinforcing the beliefs.

Step Three – Continue with the exercise by having your assistant ask, or by asking yourself:

    a.   What belief might someone have in order to

experience (insert the answer recorded earlier for *what would you like to change in your life* under *Issues* column)?

b. How would they prove that belief to be true?

c. What other belief might someone have in order to experience (insert the answer recorded earlier for *what would you like to change in your life* under *Issues* column)?

d. How would they prove that belief to be true?

Continue the exercise by alternating the two questions until a realization is brought to mind.

Here is an example of a dialogue working through the Discovering Transparent Beliefs exercise.

Step Two:

What would you like to change in your life?

Answer - "My fear of speaking publicly to large groups." (Record this answer in *Issues* column.)

Step Three:

    a. What belief might someone have in order to experience the fear of speaking publicly to large groups?

Answer - "I might say something wrong."

    b. "How would you prove that belief is true?"

Answer - "I have embarrassed myself in the past by saying something incorrectly."

    c. "What other belief might someone hold in order to experience fear of speaking publicly to large groups?"

Answer - "I am not a good public speaker.

    b. "How would you prove that belief is true?"

Answer - "The last time I spoke in public I was worried about my performance and I did not do well."

    c. "What other belief might someone have in order to experience the fear of speaking publicly to large groups?"

Answer - "I believe that people will not listen to what I

have to say."

b. "How would you prove that belief is true?"

Answer - "I felt that people were not listening to me when I last spoke. That's my Transparent Belief! I was the youngest of seven siblings. I always felt what I had to say was not important. My older brothers told me to keep quiet; no one cared what I thought. My transparent belief is 'What I have to say is not important'. I would like to change this belief."

Step Four – Record your *transparent belief* in the *Old Beliefs* column. The transparent belief will be addressed when the entire process is completed. I encourage you to use this simple exercise anytime you want to create new goals or powerful intentions.

Even if you don't get the results or revelations that you expect from this exercise use what you do receive. Use the answers and discoveries that did emerge. You can't go wrong as you ask yourself questions. You will be pleased with the results.

Practical Process Preparation

The next part of this exercise begins with the second sheet of paper. Begin by writing *New Beliefs* in the upper left side of the page. Now write *Powerful Intentions* on the upper right side of the same page.

Now that you have identified your *transparent belief* in the first exercise you can release this transparent belief. You are now able to identify the issues you want to change.

Don't give attention to your old beliefs. They are gone and will serve no purpose.

Your issues, or the things you want to change, are now addressed with your *powerful intentions*. You will no longer require these when the process is complete.

Once your new beliefs and powerful intentions are recorded on paper you may destroy the first sheet. Some people who work through this exercise find it liberating to burn the first sheet ceremonially. Some also feel the process is complete when they tear the paper to shreds or toss it into the garbage.

These old beliefs are of no use. Your newly created beliefs and intentions become the entire focus of your attention.

Practical Application

Moving forward you will use the transparent belief you discovered to create a new belief. Record the new belief on the second sheet of paper.

Keep your written record and refer to it as often as you need. You will grow comfortable in the knowledge that you own this new belief.

Next, create a powerful intention relating to, and supporting your new belief. This is your catalyst for change. This step sets your life into motion with a new series of choices, a corridor of additional doors that were not obvious prior to the creation of this powerful intention.

Step one – Under the column *New Beliefs* write your new belief in a present tense. The statement should embody your conviction. For example, *"What I have to say is important."*

Step two – Record under the column *Powerful Intentions* your powerful intention in a present tense statement. This statement should convey your purpose and the feeling you want to experience while reaching this personal goal.

Your new belief is recorded with doubtless conviction. State this belief out loud, in your own voice, after you have written it. If there is any doubt present look for additional transparent beliefs. You may wish to repeat the *Transparent Belief* exercise.

Your belief is verbalized as an undeniable fact. There should be no second thoughts or doubts. The new belief you created is unconditionally yours.

If you feel that you're getting no results from the Transparent Belief exercise don't worry. The *Belief, Intention, Choice* process will work for you even if you do not gain insights from the Transparent exercise.

Consider it a bonus if you receive helpful feedback. Use this information to assist you in furthering your move to self-empowerment.

If you return to your original negative or transparent beliefs redirect your attention to the New Belief. You may have consciously or unconsciously repeated those old beliefs to yourself hundreds of times throughout your life. You are totally unaware of the adverse results of this habit.

For example, your job required you to speak to large groups of people each month. Each time you hear your brother's voice from your childhood saying "What you have to say is not important."

Once you have created your new belief and powerful intention you will receive loud and clear choices each time the old belief resurfaces. Focus your attention on your new belief, and even more importantly, your powerful intention.

Your powerful intention will take center stage. Your belief states *what is* and your powerful intention states *what is and what is to come.*

An example, "When I regularly speak in front of large groups of people I feel connected, warm and well received."

This statement is written and spoken in the present tense. Your mind will recognize the powerful intention and respond accordingly. Appropriate choices will present themselves and assure actualization.

All your focus should be on the powerful intention. This is what sets your future into motion and brings to life your dreams and desires.

Later in the book I will guide you through the creation of more beliefs and intentions. I will provide a number of examples with different situations and issues.

It is important to continue reading the remaining chapters so you will receive a healthy understanding of the importance of the effects that beliefs, intentions and choices have on our lives, our will and our actions.

The Process in a Nutshell

The simple steps of this process are:

1. Decide what you want to change or improve in your life.

2. Discover the transparent beliefs you hold.

3. Create new empowering beliefs.

4. Create powerful intentions, propelling you forward.

5. Observe new choices and act upon them.

Don't let the simplicity of this process fool you.

It will awaken the sleeping master within and heighten your senses bringing about welcome change in your life.

I used to say "I'll believe it when I see it!" Now, I say "I'll see it when I believe it!"

Remember, belief precedes experience.

Chapter Three

What Are Beliefs and How Do They Affect Our Lives?

Belief: 1) Something believed, a connection. 2) Confidence in the truth. 3) Confidence, faith, trust

- Webster's unabridged dictionary

When a notion is converted into a solid belief, the creative power of the Universe is unleashed and the manifestation of a miracle is at hand.

We don't need to read Webster's definition to have a good idea of what a *belief* is. It is what we hold as our truth, faith and conviction.

Most of our beliefs were adopted from others early in life. We were indoctrinated with the remainder.

It is empowering to learn to create beliefs at will. Operating from knowledge of our self is where life unfolds.

Your beliefs are yours and yours alone. We may share similar beliefs about certain things but they may affect each of us differently.

Some feel their experiences shape their beliefs, while others hold to their beliefs and shape their individual experiences deliberately.

Two individuals may experience life very differently even though they hold similar beliefs.

The one who believes their experiences determine their beliefs may feel a need to constantly attempt to adapt to their environment; accepting this as a reality of their own life.

Think of a person in the water fighting the rapid current of a river.

He is desperately trying to reach the safety of the shore; instead he finds himself being swept over rocks and into tree branches, pulled back into the rapids.

All the while he believes these experiences will reinforce existing beliefs.

"The river is too strong. I cannot fight the current."

This statement is an example of disempowerment.

What if the other person relaxed, floated on her back and allowed the river to carry her on the current believing she would be carried to safety? Because she believes, her experience is such. "I always allow the river to take me safely to the shore."

Would you prefer to believe that your experiences are shaping your reality or your beliefs are shaping your reality? It would seem preferable to control beliefs allowing the world to unfold in a manner consistent with personal ideals rather than to succumb to experiences dictated by outside forces.

Life is as we make it. When we choose to operate from the perspective of the creator of our personal beliefs, empowerment is the norm. We are encouraged by the knowledge that our life's journey is our choice.

I unknowingly created a belief that my life was hard after my father's suicide. Every negative event became an opportunity to reinforce that philosophy. Every difficult experience had control on what I believed.

My dog died, life is hard.

I wrecked my car, see, life is hard!

I experienced depression; once again, my life is very hard.

My experiences were dictating my beliefs. Who is in charge here?

Years later, I discovered that I held this self-defeating belief. I made a decision to eliminate it. I changed my belief to *life is easier now and getting better all the time.*

Life became not only easier and better for me but I began to attract wonderful experiences into my life. All the old situations I considered *hard* became neutral or positive learning experiences. My new attitude left little room for life's difficulties to have lasting effects on me.

Indoctrination Anyone?

Some beliefs may not be so easily changed. Many convictions were indoctrinated into us at an early age. We were vulnerable and impressionable or they were implanted due to events in our youth. We labeled these events and created beliefs.

These certainties would serve to guide us and direct our decisions and attitudes even as we were unaware of the reasons for our decisions. Unfortunately, many undesirable beliefs ruled our subconscious. They drove us to negativity and uncertainty in our choices and attitudes.

Just to provide an example of indoctrination, let's say your parents believed that foreigners were evil thieves.

The family who resided next door to you were foreigners from a country you never even heard of. Your older brother became friends with the foreigner's daughter. Based on the *foreigners evil thieves belief* your parents disapproved of the friendship and would not allow the young woman into your home.

Your parents held a conviction that she would steal from them because she was a foreigner.

You learned this attitude at a very early age. As a result you became afraid to get to know anyone who was a foreigner for fear they would steal your lunch money. You certainly did not like the teen witch next door either!

Your brother was the only family member to avoid the permanent indoctrination. He made a decision not to adopt the belief *foreigners are evil thieves* and became a friend to the girl.

Disapproval, disappointment and disciplinary actions from parents or authority figures can result in adverse effects later in life. Beliefs can be created during early years that may trip you up in life as an adult.

Parents may discipline children harshly. They discipline by using belittling and angry words. They hold that this method of correction will result in children who think before they act. Making a mistake is a shameful act under this belief system.

People who grew up under the umbrella of fear and shame carry this attitude forward into adulthood. If they make a mistake in their job they fear retribution and shame from their boss or colleagues.

In some cases this childhood experience results in people growing to be overachievers who are very hard on themselves for any mistake. The person who is driven to perfection can have an extreme downward spiral if they hit a large roadblock in their life.

I am not judging a parent's individual method of discipline. This is an example of how beliefs are created in childhood that may cause misdirection later in life.

The good news is that at any moment of any day we can make a decision to change our belief system and experience life in a new way that's eluded us. Life is ours to create.

Believe and ye shall be…..sick!

I worked with a salesman who possessed an incredible story of the power of belief.

Dave was one of the top performing salesmen on my team. He was loved and respected by his customers and co-workers alike. One day he was giving a sales pitch to a family. As they spent time with him, Dave's customers all had flu-like symptoms. All four were coughing and sniffling throughout their encounter with Dave.

Dave came to me afterward and with great conviction he stated that he would be sick the next day. I asked him why he thought that. He told me that he could actually *feel* their germs attacking his sinuses and lungs as he was in close proximity with the ill family.

"Dave, you could not possibly feel the germs attacking you within minutes of being in the company of these people," I said.

He replied, "Honest to God, I could feel the germs actually attacking me right then. I know that I will be sick in the morning."

When I asked Dave not to set himself up to be sick, he told me there was no doubt in his mind that he would be. The process had already begun.

First thing the next morning Dave came straight to my office. He looked miserably ill.

"See, I told you I would be sick! Those people made me sick!"

I truly wished he had understood the power that he held within his grasp to control his self-fulfilling prophecy. If we can make ourselves ill that easily, can we also heal ourselves with that level of belief?

Fear at the Canyon Rim

When I was a teenager my brother, Van would take friends to a place he visited near Andrew College in Cuthbert, Georgia. Providence Canyon State Park, or Little Grand Canyon as some call it, is a wonderful location to hike.

Van discovered Providence Canyon State Park when he attended Andrew College before my father's death. The canyon walls are approximately 150 feet at the deepest point. It is a striking, beautiful and unexpected location to see in the hills of western Georgia.

Van, his best friend Mike and I made the trip together to hike the trails and climb the canyon walls. I had a fear of heights and was trying to overcome it. Van and Mike found difficult places to climb from the floor of the canyon to the rim. We spent hours attempting maneuvers that required a great deal of thought and cooperation, not to mention courage.

I lacked courage, although there were times when they

convinced me to join them and we made a successful climb. That was exhilarating!

I decided to break away from Van and Mike. They were tackling more and more difficult routines and I was afraid to make the climbs.

I moved to an area of the canyon where it was approximately 100 feet deep. As I created a plan for my solo climb I noticed a root protruding from the canyon rim. It was parallel to the ground and jutted upwards a foot at the end, like a giant fish hook. It looked sturdy and a good place for me to pull myself over the edge of the rim.

I surveyed the area below carefully then mapped the course in my mind. I began at a point to the right of the root and made my way upwards.

I felt the need to prove myself to my fellow climbers and for my ego as well.

The path I chose was relatively safe except for a couple of very tight places. If I slipped I would have slipped over the edge and plummeted about 90 feet down to the muddy bottom. I took my time, proceeding with caution, even though my fear of heights was in full gear.

With great trepidation I approached the root on a steadily narrowing ledge. My heart was pounding as never before. I was within a few feet of the rim but the gripping fear of slipping and falling to my death was in the forefront of my mind.

Somehow I overcame the fear long enough to stretch my arm out to grasp the root and pull myself up to it. I was perched on the tip of the twelve inch wide ledge. I had a death lock on the root, wrapping both my arms around it. I stood on the ledge, holding tight to the root which was at shoulder's level.

All I had to do was pull myself onto the root and and make my way up and over the edge. My head was 12" from the canyon rim. This was an easy task, especially after the difficult climb to arrive at this point.

But there I stood, planning my moves, evaluating the circumstances and trying to envision myself celebrating at the top.

I clung to the root, paralyzed, for fifteen tortuous minutes.

I was agonizing over the decision to pull myself up and over the edge, or descend back down to the bottom and join the others. The more I considered it, the more doubt and fear overcame me. I began to visualize the fall to the bottom, rather than the successful climb over the rim and to the top.

Nearly in tears, and feeling sick with guilt for letting myself down, I capitulated and made my way back down. I was disappointed in myself even though it was a very difficult and dangerous maneuver that could have crippled or killed me had I fallen.

I was much harder on myself than I should have been. Later, I told Van and Mike that I had almost made it over the edge but the terrain was too difficult and I was amazed I had even gotten that far.

I could not bear to tell them how disappointed I was in myself.

I have thought of that instance frequently over the years. I believed that I did not have the courage to make it to the top and that my behavior proved that to be true.

However, it may very well have been latent good judgment on my part. Who knows, the root could have snapped off and sent me plummeting to the canyon floor.

It's also possible that I could have discovered right then that I held a belief that I did not have the courage to complete the climb and then proceed to rid myself of it.

I may have been able to replace that *lack of courage belief* with a new belief that would have enabled me to make it up and over the ledge.

As the saying goes, "if I only knew then what I know now," the outcome may have been different.

It is a testament to the power of belief. As we believe, so it is. I wanted to make it to the top but my belief stood in the way.

We adopt or create all our own beliefs. We can create new beliefs to replace those we hold. Once we accept this truth we are on the road to self-liberation and the development of convictions that are empowering.

It's More Than an Attitude

A positive attitude definitely makes a difference but it is the belief that ultimately overrules the attitude. I can be positive that an overabundance of money will come to me if I remain open to it. However, if I have an underlying belief that money is the root of all evil then I may just receive enough money to get by.

It takes much more than a positive attitude to navigate our way through life. I utilized positive affirmations and mantras for many years and they made a tremendous difference in my life. Nothing engendered effective change as much as eliminating the disempowering beliefs and creating new positive beliefs with powerful intentions.

It's the best formula that I have encountered. This combination has created a massive shift in my ability to control my world.

We are here to create the lives we desire. We are here to experience life as we choose.

I have chosen to create joy, happiness, bliss and the fulfillment of my personal dreams. Each step we take, each time we give ourselves the opportunity to move forward toward our highest expectation and dreams is an exciting moment.

Empowerment is within our grasp. It is available to all who will decide to embrace it.

If I decided to run a marathon and I entered into training with a negative, defeatist attitude, how prepared would I actually be to participate in the run? Would I complete the race? Would I perform to the best of my ability?

What if I held a positive, empowered attitude as I began training? Would I perform at higher levels and achieve greater results? More than likely so!

A positive attitude will help keep one focused and feeling good; but a positive belief combined with a powerful intention will set the game into motion.

More doors of opportunity will be opened once the intention is set. The mind goes about searching for ways to accomplish its task. It looks for all available possibilities. As the possibilities present themselves we recall our intention and make choices that will help lead to the attainment of our goals.

You are about to enjoy a homemade pot roast with garlic mashed potatoes on the side.

The pot roast is delicious, and the garlic mashed potatoes are fantastic on their own. They would all taste even better with rich, brown gravy ladled over the top.

The meat and potatoes are beliefs and the gravy is the positive attitude.

The pot roast and potatoes, (or beliefs) are more palatable because of the gravy, (the positive attitude) that was added to them.

A positive attitude would not be enjoyed or as effective unless it was accompanied by beliefs. This makes for an enjoyable, practical and powerful combination.

A positive attitude is a plus and a must, but it also must have something for it to enhance to be utilized to the fullest.

A belief says, "This is the way it is."

A positive attitude says, "It is this way, I like it and what can I do to make it happen or make it better?"

What If?

What would the world be like if we all held the same beliefs? What if everyone believed that we are all peaceful people, we are all here to share with each other and to assist each other in any way we can?

Sounds like a great world, doesn't it?

What if everyone also believed that we did not need liners in our landfills, we could dump all waste, including nuclear waste, in the oceans and streams. What if everyone believed that it is ok to hunt and fish any plant or animal to extinction?

What would our world be like then?

How about a world where all people had no belief system? Is that even possible? Is there anything you can conceive of in this physical or subjective world that does not relate to a belief?

Think about that for a moment.

Think of a cloud in the sky. If you see it, do you believe it is there? Do you believe that it is a cloud? Do you believe the cloud has the propensity to provide rain or shade? Do you believe the cloud is moving across the sky?

What about a joyful thought, do you believe it because you feel it? Do you feel joy because you believe it? Do you believe it is actually joy and you can share the experience?

I cannot think of anything that is not related to a belief. If it is within your sight or your consciousness do you accept and believe it is real?

Or perhaps you believe it is not there, which sounds like another sort of belief.

One more "what if"?

What if everyone in the world believed that they could eliminate any belief that was not serving them well and replace it with a new belief?

They could chose to create a belief that would empower them and move them forward to their personal goals and dreams.

What would our world be like then?

What would your world be like then?

Imagine releasing the beliefs that are hindering your spiritual growth, slowing your financial progress or interrupting your emotional expression.

Beliefs can interfere with personal relationships and our perception of ourselves. Once we are free from the clutter of negativity it allows us to create positive and empowering beliefs. New convictions change the way we experience situations in our life. We are open to new beginnings and fresh possibilities.

Recognizing and eliminating negative beliefs is an act of liberation.

Many people are not free to express their beliefs. We are blessed with the freedom to believe as we choose. We are also blessed with the ability to use our minds to create and eliminate thoughts and beliefs.

Changed Your Filter Lately?

Beliefs are the filters through which we perceive all events and experiences in our lives. Are beliefs good or bad?

Yes, they are; just as you believe them to be. Beliefs can be enabling or disabling, depending on your personal assessment.

For example, a young man has three auto accidents in a single year. He professes to his family and friends, "I am a really bad driver. I have car wrecks all of the time."

Is holding this belief helpful or harmful? It's certainly not helpful, even if the belief is true.

By changing his assertion he may have a better chance of avoiding future mishaps. It would serve him well to create a new belief, such as, "I feel better now being a safe, aware driver. I am constantly improving my driving skills."

If he follows up his new belief with an intention to improve his driving habits he may be able to experience a new reality of being a safe, accident free driver.

The young driver's beliefs must be in *alignment* with his

intentions and his actions. His actions will be determined by the choices he makes.

Let's take a quick look at Webster's second definition of the word *alignment*. The driver's beliefs should be in a state of agreement or cooperation with his cause or intention. This will produce the desired effect or result.

Alignment: 1) An adjustment to a line, arrangement in a straight line. 2) a state of agreement or cooperation among persons, (yourself) grounds, nations, etc. with a common cause or viewpoint (intention).

- Webster's Unabridged Dictionary

Once he rids himself of his old belief and successfully creates a new positive belief the young driver should then create a powerful intention. This intention will serve the belief by propelling him forward and opening him to choices that lead him to fulfillment.

What's In Your Belief Bank?

Old beliefs may come back to haunt us. In the prior example the young driver created a new belief. What if every time he gets behind the wheel that old belief, "I'm a bad driver" comes to mind?

After years of accepting this belief as gospel it may very well be the first thing that comes to his mind. The thought must be recognized and labeled as an old belief. Attention will then be transferred to the new belief. He will return to the new belief each time old thoughts surface.

It's like having coins stored in a gallon jar. Your ceramic jar has a large opening. The only change you've saved over the year is pennies. The jar is half full of pennies. Occasionally you reach in and grab a handful of pennies to spend.

Gradually you decide to toss in nickels and dimes because they are of greater value. Each time you return to the jar your hand comes out with pennies and a few nickels and dimes.

The nickels and dimes were the last thing to be saved in the jar, so they're the first to be retrieved.

Then you decide that quarters would be the best denomination to save. They are now the only coins you add to the savings jar.

After a few weeks of saving quarters you dive into the jar and grab a handful of coins; a few pennies, several nickels and dimes and a few quarters.

The old pennies are still coming through, but fewer and fewer find their way into your hand. They are now further from the surface. The greater the quantity of valuable coins you put into the ceramic jar the further the pennies move from the surface.

Months later, after diligent saving, you reach into your bank and a wonderful thing happens. You draw out a handful of quarters. It feels great knowing that your most valuable beliefs, (I mean coins), are now the most accessible. The old beliefs, (I mean worthless pennies), are now completely out of sight.

If all you have is pennies, (old negative beliefs), in your bank that is all you will access from your jar.

It's really quite simple, each time an old belief rears its ugly head just turn your attention to your new belief. Put your focus on it and keep it there. Before long you will be amazed at how infrequently you think about an old belief.

Dennis Waitley once said, "We move in the direction of our currently most dominant thoughts."

What thoughts are predominant in your mind? We want positive, solid and worthwhile beliefs dominating our thoughts so we move toward them.

While working I sometimes realize I'm tapping my foot to music playing in another room.

Subconsciously I have been listening to the music while working.

If our old negative reel to reel is playing constantly in the background we may be unknowingly moving to that old beat, falling into its rhythm. It's time to bring the digital player out and play new positive background music. Allow it to dominate our minds.

Is Your Ship Seaworthy?

One element of the *Chaos Theory* is the Law of Sensitive Dependence on Initial Conditions, more commonly known as the *Butterfly Effect*.

The *Chaos Theory* was born out of a revolutionary perspective on natural phenomena. Reference is made to the fact that massive change occurs as a result of an extremely minute variation over a period of time.

Recall the story of a ship at sea. The ship's bearing is off by only one degree on the compass. Continuing on this course, the ship's final destination will be several hundred miles off.

What if one's belief is like the ship? Their intention is the engine powering that ship and their choices are the degree markers on the compass. The ship, or belief, is sound. The engine, or intention, is propelling the ship properly. The single problem is with the compass' degree markers, our analogy for choices. The wrong choice was made for the bearing. As time passes the destination will not be reached.

I can own a solid belief and feel its worth to me. I can also establish the most powerful intention that I desire to complete. However, each time I make a choice that does not support the intention my journey is either delayed or altered. If I do not correct my course by making the right choices my intention may never be realized.

It's the synchronistic approach that solidifies the process. Each element is dependent upon the other.

When a positive belief is created and is in alignment with an established intention and the right choices are made thereafter, any goal will stand a far greater chance of being achieved.

There are unforeseen catastrophes, storms and difficulties that arise along the journey interfering, interrupting or ending the adventure. This is where you may tweak the intentions or make alternate choices. Use your will to put forth more effort with your actions.

Right beliefs + right intentions + right choices add up to the right destination.

Chapter Four

Are Your Intentions Powerful?

Intention: 1) An act or instance of determining mentally upon some action or result. 2) The end or object intended, purpose. 3) Purpose or attitude toward the effect of one's actions or conduct.

- Webster's Unabridged Dictionary

We were born out of the ultimate expression of creation through the intention of the Universe, the will of God, if you prefer. We were intended into being. It is this same will, this exact Divine expression of intention that exists within all humans.

If we were created in the image of God as creator then we too are creators. We are responsible for creating much of the world we live in.

Man has created incredible things. Just look around and admire the beauty and creativity of the arts, music, dance, food, architecture and gardens. Appreciate the value of transportation, the internet, television, communication and computer networks among many of man's inventions.

We are endowed with the seeds of inspiration. These seeds sprout forth at some point to fall under the direction of the power of our intentions.

Our intentions move us forward, and lead us to the choices that lie before us fueling the will to move us beyond our self-imposed limitations.

We are born to create. We live in a world that thrives from creative Source. It is all as we create it to be; the good, the bad and the ugly. Our intentions serve to foster change, good or bad change. It is our birthright to use the gift of creativity to our soul's desire.

When we wish to create change in a behavior or situation an intention moves us toward our goal. The belief is the basis point to operate from but it is the intention that ultimately carries us toward our goal.

Why Is Intention Important?

Intention is paramount in our lives. It is our driving force, our goal setting mechanism and our creative outlet. Intention drives us to design, create and complete our dreams and desires. Without intention our lives would be meaningless and quite boring. What would life be like without the desire to live a dream, attain a goal or move in the direction of our inclinations?

There is a significant difference between an intention and a powerful intention.

An intention is what I can visualize myself doing. A powerful intention is put into writing with thought and feeling. It has enough thought and feeling behind it assuring that additional and better choices become available that will lead to the realization of the intention.

A powerful intention is in alignment with our belief and uses our will to bring it to fruition. A powerful intention says, "This is what I set out to do," and looks for the best possible choices that are conducive to the accomplishment of the goal.

Many people would like to change a habit or situation. They either lack the impetus or are unaware of a method that they feel comfortable and confident utilizing.

Perhaps someone impulsively overspends each time they go to the grocery story. They return home with not only much more than they intended, but with a few things they do not need. This person would like to change this habit but does not know how. They experience remorse each time they overspend. They feel powerless as they are compulsively drawn to spend.

The impulse spender may have sought help from books, media sources or the Internet, with no success. It is possible that the only thing they were lacking was a powerful intention.

A person must recognize that they are facing an issue that is important enough to them or they have experienced stress or anxiety as a result of the situation and they finally make the issue a priority. They must handle it with whatever means is necessary to effect immediate change.

A person will not change because they want change or need change. A person will only change when they are *ready* to change.

What Makes Intention Work?

Commitment! Commitment to our cause, to our goal, to our dream is what makes intention work. When we finally are committed to changing our habits or situation we will turn our life into what we want it to be. Life then becomes truly rewarding and exciting.

If you want to become the CEO of a major corporation and you are currently working on the sales floor, you must create a powerful intention, back it up with a strong belief and commit yourself to learning and applying what it takes to become the CEO.

Just 'wanting' the position is not enough to make it happen.

Once the belief and intention are created and recorded in writing, your choices and options will become glaringly obvious to you. Writing your powerful intention in a journal or simply on a piece of paper is the first action step in this process. There will naturally be more options and choices available because it is not just a fleeting whim, it is a powerful desire put into place by a powerful means of moving toward your goal.

Intention works when we allow ourselves to become involved at a deeper level. When we invoke our deepest desires and dreams and feed them with the fuel of commitment there will be nothing that can stand in our way, besides our own self.

Creating a pure and true intention becomes a catalyst to fulfilling the dreams that we hold dear to our heart. When we succeed in fulfilling our dreams we move the whole of humanity to the next level of being.

When we utilize our creative source to advance our state of being and move us toward our highest good then we also move mankind toward its highest good.

We are one small part of the whole. Every decision we make and every intention we fulfill makes a difference to the whole, no matter how small we perceive it to be.

Goal Setters Make Better Lovers

It is interesting to note how important goal setting is in the business world and how much effort goes into creating and achieving those goals.

One thing that is, and has always been, consistent with the most successful companies in the world is the importance they've placed on setting goals.

Many organizations set annual, monthly or daily goals. They develop five or ten year long-range plans.

It has been well documented that goals drive companies to success. Without goals businesses would find themselves floundering in a sea of competition. Clear and concise goals make the difference in how a company performs and what level of success they will achieve.

When I was a general sales manager I received a DOC, (daily operating control).

The DOC showed me our sales in each department, the gross profits and unexpected expenses or chargebacks that accrued through that day.

I always knew where we stood compared with our forecasts or goals. I could adjust our advertising, incentives or workload to accommodate the sales pace we were tracking.

Would it not be even more important to have personal goals of your own?

We would have the tools to assess our success. If we have no goals in our life then we have little or no direction and the slightest hiccup can throw us off track.

A powerful intention can withstand the unexpected blows that sometimes come with life's changes.

Strengthen your position in life. Create some excitement with worthwhile goals that when achieved will bring satisfaction and fulfillment.

Walking the Fire

For many years I was intrigued by those who have walked on fire and endured the burning coals seemingly by miraculous underpinnings. A decade ago I became more interested due to the empowering nature of this feat. I was compelled to learn more about fire walks.

I considered participating in Tony Robbins' seminars involving firewalking. I twice almost signed up but began to doubt myself and decided not to attend at the last minute. I tried to enlist co-workers and friends to join me, but no one was interested enough to follow through.

I *wanted* to attempt firewalking, but I later realized that I had beliefs that were standing in my way.

It was recurring self-doubt that plagued me at times. After a few years of disappointments I finally decided that it was up to me. No one stood in my way except myself.

My favorite mantra, one I learned at an Avatar conference, is "I am as I decide to be."

So, I decided to be brave and allow the Universe to hold my hand as I sought out a firewalk ceremony to attend.

I wanted to conquer my doubts and believe in higher possibilities for myself. This would be one more step of liberation and self-empowerment that was a dream of mine for so many years. I was ready to make this firewalk experience my powerful intention.

In 2007 I viewed a Tampa, Florida news station's report of a firewalking ceremony. The reporter attended the ceremony, actually participating in firewalking.

He mentioned that it was the most amazing experience. He

felt it had changed him. I researched the source and ultimately scheduled my first firewalk on April 26, 2008 near Floral City, Florida.

I discovered that I held disabling beliefs that were preventing me from attending firewalks. My beliefs included, "I am afraid of what others may think of me if I fail" and "I am not ready to walk the fire because I doubt myself" and also "I am afraid of burning myself" not to mention "I lack confidence in the Universe to protect me."

These debilitating beliefs were holding me hostage to a life of uncertainty and fear. I was allowing them to control my destiny and gave the belief power over me. This was not the way of the Divine nature within me.

This was the way of doubt, weakness and a total lack of respect for the Universe.

Wood, Glass, Arrows, Boards, Steel and Fire

That night began with the instructor sharing his past experiences with firewalking and preparatory remarks for the evening's events. There were more exercises scheduled than I was aware of. I became very excited about each one.

The attendees numbered about twenty, ranging in age from twelve to sixty-five.

The youngest was a boy attending with his parents. He was quite eager to participate in the events. He performed each with alacrity.

The instructor was very clear in his remarks about participating in the exercise. He made sure to convey that each event was optional. He went so far as to say that if there was any uneasiness or doubt present in anyone's mind they should not complete the exercises.

There was never any coaxing or even encouraging. If one felt confident about the exercise then they would participate. It was an open invitation and the props were available to those willing to participate.

Wood

Our first task as a group was to stack the hardwood. The cedar had been shipped from the western United States. Most pieces were two feet long and ten inches thick. We began the stacking process with a ceremonial blessing. We laid the wood in a box pattern stacked four feet high and eight feet long. The fire was lit. It would burn for at least two hours.

The group of participants gathered in a seminar room, seated in a circle. One side of the room was open to the outdoors. It was a beautiful, mild evening in the lightly wooded retreat. Pictures adorned one wall, displaying many firewalks with people walking and standing in the smoldering coals. Some pictures celebrated walks of record lengths, over 200 feet on the coals.

It was inspirational to say the least.

Glass

For the first exercise our instructor brought out a large wheeled case filled with broken glass. He poured the contents on a plastic mat then spread the shards evenly. The broken pieces consisted of many different types and colors of broken bottles. I was aware of this exercise; walking barefoot across the shards of glass.

There were gasps and comments in the room as the glass

was spread before us. It was an intimidating sight, but exciting as well. The prospect of walking on broken glass was inviting.

The first volunteer was a middle-aged woman. She walked across the glass barefoot, flanked by assistants. They were there to help in her exit the glass carpet if she wished. The glass crackled and broke beneath her with popping sounds. Some observing her cringed at the sound. She completed the walk without a scratch. She received thunderous applause from everyone.

I walked the glass next and it was invigorating. My heart was pounding with excitement and delight as I slowly managed each step carefully with as little thought as I could give it.

I heard glass breaking under the weight of my body. I began to experience a feeling of exhilaration and freedom. It was a fantastic start to an incredible evening of self-exploration.

Arrows

Target arrows were brought out next. I recalled reading of them being used as props in some motivational seminars. These were standard target arrows, solid wood, with a rounded, but slightly pointed tip.

The point resembled the nose of a rocket booster from the Space Shuttle. Participants were invited to place the tip of the arrow in the soft spot just below the Adam's apple, at the base of the neck. The other end of the arrow was placed against the wall.

We were instructed to walk into the wall, with no hesitation. The goal was to break the arrow. As with the broken glass exercise, not everyone volunteered. Some really struggled with the exercise and could not complete it.

If participants attempted walking to the wall with the arrow at the throat without the belief they could break it; or if they hesitated or pushed slowly the arrow created pressure against the soft spot causing pain.

The arrows were designed to break with a few pounds of pressure which would cause no harm if done with a quick, forward motion.

The key was to act without doubt, moving forward quickly with a single step believing the arrow would break. To the amazement of everyone the arrows broke. The exercise served to build confidence for the upcoming firewalk.

Boards

The next exercise was familiar to me. I found it quite elementary, but rewarding. I have broken many boards and stacks of bricks throughout my 20 years of martial arts training. For those with no training in the martial arts it can be an intimidating affair. I shared the excitement with those that broke their first twelve inch square pine board with their hands.

A stand was erected from two large concrete blocks set eleven inches apart with the board placed on top of them. A narrow edge of the board was placed on each block. The individual leaned over the stand and broke the board by striking it with the palm of the hand in a downward motion.

This was another confidence building exercise.

Steel

The next confidence building exercise was a bit tricky. The earlier arrow routine seemed like child's play compared to the next event.

A six foot piece of 3/8 inch steel rebar was brought out for the most challenging exercise of the evening. This drill was done with a partner. Each person folded a dollar bill into a one and a half inch square. The folded money was placed, again, in the soft spot at the base of the throat to prevent the rebar from cutting the flesh.

The pair faced each other, placing each end of the rebar on each other's soft spot, padded only by the folded currency.

They must walk towards each other, without using their hands, bending the rebar in half as they approach each other. Keeping in mind, the rebar is fairly rigid and sagged only a half inch at the center. It took quite a bit more effort to bend than I realized.

The instructor and a volunteer demonstrated the procedure with success, but with more effort than anyone expected. Following the demonstration two participants gave it a shot, but were unsuccessful with the task.

A woman who seemed to hold self-doubt decided to try. However, with several attempts she failed. She began to cough due to the pressure of the rebar against her throat. After four attempts many observers became concerned. She finally opted out of the exercise. Due to this uncomfortable episode no one else volunteered except a gentleman and me.

I was determined to complete all the preparatory exercises to assure my success with the firewalk. My partner and I stood face to face with the rebar between us. We knew we must not think about the process, just act *quickly* and *decisively*. We must step forward, in faith, knowing that the rebar would bend as we moved toward each other. We cleared our minds and locked our eyes together, and attempted the critical first step.

To our surprise the rebar did not bend. We struggled for a moment, then the pain became too great to continue. We realized that we'd become distracted. We were concentrating on the difficulties experienced by the previous participant and began to doubt ourselves.

My partner and I spoke for a moment and decided not to *try* again, but to *do* it this time. No hesitation and no doubts.

We would let nothing into our minds and allow our gaze to be fixed on each other's eyes; moving toward each other to complete the drill.

Incredibly, without hesitation, we placed the bar back on the dollar bills and instantly walked toward each other; bending the rebar, almost end to end. We bent the rebar in half, stopping inches from each other. What elation!

A feeling of being *unstoppable* came over me!

I was now ready to walk the fire.

The process was about quieting the mind and allowing the events to unfold and complete themselves with no resistance, no struggle and no doubt. Wouldn't it be nice to live each day and experience every obstacle in our lives like this?

Fire

Alas, the moment of truth.

We exited the room and congregated at the huge mounds of burning coals. Again, we were reminded that we should walk the coals only if we felt the movement of our spirit to do so. All participants first prepared the area for the walk. We spread the coals the width and length of the firewalk path.

The path was approximately fifteen feet long, enough to make four or five steps through the burning embers. The instructor measured the temperature of the coals with an infrared thermometer and reported the temperature was 1,100 degrees.

We worked together preparing the coals, sharing a single rake. Each of us lasted ten seconds before passing on the rake. The incredible heat explained our inability to work longer than a few seconds. It felt as if your face would blister if you worked longer. Several of the attendees decided not to walk the fire.

The smoldering embers and heat were intimidating to say

the least.

The coals were spread and the moment was at hand. The instructor gave us a chant to recite as we circled the fire. As each person felt ready, they walked the coals.

It was simultaneously exhilarating, joyous and peaceful. Each person who walked the coals celebrated the moment with all of us.

It truly was a joyous occasion. We felt a bond that was inspirational. I, along with the parents of the twelve year old boy experienced such a feeling of triumph when he walked the coals. His success inspired me to walk the fire again and yet, again, a third time.

Everyone returned to the conference room where the instructor gave us note cards and asked us to write "I walked on fire. I can do anything I want."

It was to be a reminder of the miraculous event that we participated in. The note card was to remind us of how we went far beyond the limits of our beliefs. How we can use our intentions to move us forward in the direction of our innermost desires. It was to remind us of how we manifest our dreams and goals at will.

It is our powerful intentions that serve to bring about the desired changes that we wish to see in our lives. The power of our intentions is greater than any passing thought. It is greater than the *want to* or the *I'd like to*. It becomes the *I am now ready for* that makes the creation manifest.

The Thirteen Year Garden

Paula and I moved into the house where we now reside over thirteen years ago. In our first days in our new home we were determined to have a vegetable garden.

My wife and I designed the house and had it built on an acre of land. There is plenty of room for a garden. We bought wooden fence sections *before we even built the house.*

Now that's intention! Well, it was intention, but there was no power behind it. It was a weak, half-hearted effort to create a worthwhile goal.

Paula and I discussed it many times through the years. We

even designed the garden on paper.

Why did it not come to fruition?

We had plenty of excuses. We were busy with life, raising children, working a job, hobbies and projects, social activities and more.

It was merely procrastination! We still desired a garden. It was not until I began writing this book that I realized how simple it would be to actually create the powerful intention and get our garden started!

I realized there were beliefs holding me hostage.

"I don't have time for a garden."

"It's too much work."

"I don't know enough about gardening to succeed."

Our garden was safely locked away in our *Someday* dreams.

I am happy to say the garden is now a reality. I found time each week to devote to creating the garden. I handled the large amount of effort and work required. I have learned enough along the way to make it a reality.

Were it not for creating a new belief and a powerful intention to bring this garden into existence, the weeds would still overtake that section of our yard. It was incredibly exciting seeing the progress each week; it was satisfying watching the original dream manifest several days before my intended date of completion.

Much of the excitement and satisfaction of the garden's creation has been carried forward by our family and friends. They view the garden's progress each week. Our friends and neighbors, Tim and Sue, are contributing as well, looking forward to sharing the garden's bounty with us. We each enjoy the rewarding experience as we toil in the sun together; moving toward a common goal.

Many thoughts entered my mind each week about the garden and what I need to do to accomplish the task. I realized what needed to be done to stay on track. Choices became evident.

The choices I decided to make during the week determined whether I stayed on track. If I decided to watch television more than I should, or read books unrelated to gardening I was delaying knowledge needed for the next step in the garden. I would have lost pace and delayed my date of the completion of my goal.

The beautiful garden was designed by my wife, Paula. It is located in the sunniest part of our yard, just beyond the oak trees. The center features a large cement planter raised eighteen inches within a ring of cylindrical terracotta tiles. These tiles are positioned to stack vertically in a circle, forming two levels of raised beds where herbs are planted.

Extending from the center in a cross pattern is a walkway of broken cement pieces laid together in a mosaic feature. Connecting the four points of the cross is a diamond shaped path of stepping stones dividing the planting beds.

Paula's design is a square surrounding a diamond and centered inside is a Celtic cross. It is beautiful.

I have planted onions, peppers, lettuce, spinach, cilantro, chives, parsley, dill, oregano, lemon balm and tomatoes.

As I write this it is November in Florida. I will watch for the occasional frost but usually one or two evenings of covering the delicate plants will protect them. We have many more vegetables to plant and a few more herbs. We are already planning for our spring crop.

Intentions should be powerful, more than just wants or desires for something. If our intentions are something that we truly wish to accomplish or obtain then we need to avail ourselves of the very best opportunities and choices. Only that will bring the intentions to reality, creating a powerful intention, not just a wish list.

The attainment of our intentions brings joy to our lives. Without powerful intentions our lives could be dull. We won't experience life to the fullest.

Our intentions do not need to be self-serving. We may have a strong desire to serve others. We may wish to assist our local or global community, but have never followed through and made the commitment to serve.

When we actually make this commitment and create an intention to help others, the world becomes a bit better because we have acted upon our intentions powerfully and deliberately.

Once a belief is conceived, without doubts, and a powerful

intention is created with the full support of the will, the intention will either manifest immediately *or a path will be revealed that leads to fulfillment along with one or more choices.*

The Universe (God, Source, Divine, Supreme Being…) is not on our schedule. Our idea of manifesting desires immediately may not be what the Universe will provide.

I once read an article which included an interesting analogy of a boomerang and the Universe.

Your powerful intention is like the boomerang. You toss it out into the Universe. It may come back to you immediately or it may take a long loop around and come back days, weeks or even years later. All the important or inconsequential choices you make during the boomerang's loop may determine the time frame of its manifestation.

It may not manifest immediately. Between our timing and the Universe's timing the creation will ultimately either manifest in our reality due to the actions and choices we have made or it will dissipate altogether as a result of our inability to maintain focus and commit to our goal.

Our will must be engaged and our intentions honorable and powerful enough to see it through to completion.

When we create an intention and believe in it as a reality our choices of success are greatly enhanced. As creative beings we begin with thoughts and then move into creating ideas, desires, intentions and outcomes with our minds. The very act of creation places it soundly in the Universe within the realms of the time space configuration. It may not be visible or recognizable yet, however, it is there somewhere awaiting the opportunity to come into being.

A new life awaits each of us at any given moment. We may ratchet up the excitement and joy in our lives by utilizing the power of intention. It is a power that can move us beyond the limitations we sometimes imprison ourselves with.

Make a commitment to use your gift of intention in a way that pleases you and benefits your world.

Your powerful intention can make the difference between just living a day to day life or living a life of passion, bliss and excitement.

Chapter Five

Exactly How Important Are the Choices We Make?

Choice: 1) An act or instance of choosing, selection. 2) The right, power or opportunity to choose, option. 3) A person or thing chosen or eligible to be chosen. 4) An alternative. 5) An abundance or variety from which to choose.

- Webster's Unabridged Dictionary

The instant we make a choice the path we and others are on is altered.

You have stopped your automobile at an intersection of a busy highway. You are waiting for the light to turn green. As the light changes, you pause to take a sip of coffee before proceeding through the green light. The car in the lane next to you doesn't hesitate. The driver immediately accelerates through the green light moving directly into the path of a speeding truck. The car to adjacent to you is hit broadside and totaled by the red light runner.

If you had made the choice to postpone the sip of coffee and hit the gas when the light changed to green your car would have propelled into the path of the truck, instead a stranger's life was affected by your choice.

We make hundreds of choices each day. The seemingly insignificant choices that we make every minute of each day may amount to much greater consequences than we can imagine.

Rise and Shine!

Think about your day as it begins. You alarm clock sounds waking you for the day. Your first decision is whether you will turn off the alarm, or not.

You are sleepy. It would feel good to lie in bed, under the covers, a while longer. You quickly tire of the sound of the alarm. You reach for the clock. Then think perhaps you should hit the Snooze button instead. Next your decision becomes whether you truly want to sleep a bit longer or get up immediately. Do you need to get to the office a few minutes early today? If so, what part of your morning routine will need to change?

You make the decision to get up now and realize your choice is to turn your alarm off from the snooze setting. Are you going to put on house slippers as you rise from bed? You know that the floor is cold and hard. You put on your slippers and as you stand more choices present themselves.

Should you start the coffee pot immediately, or detour by the bathroom first? Are you sure you want to begin the day with coffee? Should you wait for your first cup when you arrive at work, or possibly stop for a cup on the drive to your job? Should you add a quick breakfast if you make a stop for coffee?

You detour by the restroom to sort out your morning nourishment choices.

Later you head for the kitchen, you've decided on home brewed coffee. Your mouth is dry. Should you first get a glass of water? Splash water or your face, or even drink water from the faucet as you splash your face?

You're chilled, should you reach for your robe or the

thermostat to increase the warmth?

There have been quite a few choices you have faced within a few moments. There could be many others during the same period of time, such as should you straighten your crooked shirt? Your ear itches, will you scratch it or ignore it? This list could go on.

Many choices are simply unconscious actions. They are made in rapid fire succession without awareness, yet they're choices just the same.

We are used to making decisions on demand. We may never consider the consequences of these decisions.

Let's examine the consequence of the choice to take a sip of coffee at the red light. Was there thought in this action to delay the procession through the intersection? Was the delay a result of a deliberate decision to drink the coffee?

Was the sip an automated response of the desire to quench your thirst or could it have been more than that? Is it possible that this impulse arose from a deeper level of feeling or intuition? Did the driver in the vehicle hit by the truck have the same opportunity to respond to an intuitive feeling that may have prevented the collision?

Choices can be made from the rational, thinking mind or the feeling intuitive mind. Either can be correct; either can move you forward on your path toward achieving your goals.

At times we make quick, rational decisions, (the light is green, go!) or we make decisions from a deeper, more focused state of the intuitive mind, (I feel like I should take a sip of coffee before I proceed through the green light.)

It seems reasonable to at least attempt to listen to the quiet, intuitive voice within. This may seem foreign or difficult, perhaps just slowing down a bit to contemplate the available choices at hand. Being aware of atmosphere or surroundings may be a benefit. This was a concept I learned through years of martial arts training. Always be aware of your surroundings.

Look, listen and observe your feelings in all situations.

It Was Right on the Tip of My…..Finger

One of the great passions in my life is cooking. When I was much younger I spent a few years in the restaurant business; later became a wine consultant. I am a weekend chef. I enjoy sharing wine dinners with family and friends. My wife is an excellent cook; likewise my brother is fantastic with food and wine.

While preparing maduro (ripe) plantains for a Jamaican style jerk chicken pastry dish I picked up a knife that was too small. I was uncomfortable using it; however I was hurrying through the preparation and ignored the voice in my head saying that I should reach for a different knife.

Ten seconds later I sliced the tip of my finger. Immediately I said, "Why in the world didn't I listen to the warning?"

I knew I had made the wrong choice. I had been given the opportunity to avert the negative outcome.

This is an example of hearing the intuitive mind but instead choosing to succumb to the thinking mind.

The intuitive mind always respects our decisions. It will allow the consequences to unfold based on the choices we make.

Sometimes people make good choices when they are rushed for deadlines or under enormous stress. Others do not fare well. Some people are quite open to the leading of the intuitive mind. They do not allow circumstances to dictate the outcome. These individuals may enjoy the rush of adrenaline of stressful situations and make the best choices during stressful times.

Individuals who react to stress and try to think their way through it may not always make the right choices. They cannot think clearly when they experience adrenaline overload clouding their mind.

This is what happened to me when I cut my finger. I usually utilize my intuition resulting in the better choice. My actions relating to my injury is an example of how quickly one can deviate from the path, ignoring the advice of the higher self.

I am certainly not an intuitive genius, always making the best choices at will. However, there are times when I am amazed while experiencing the process unfold in its purest state. These optimum alternate choices are always available when we are feeling into the moment intuitively.

There is an incredible sense of being in flow with Divine order during these moments. This experience is not only extremely satisfying, but humbling as well.

Almost daily I find myself wondering why I just made a wrong choice. I recognize that I must face the consequences of my lack of attention. I see or hear the choices available to me. I know in my heart the right decision, but somehow I elect to be guided by my ego instead.

A coworker could playfully insult me. The innocent remark may strike a sensitive place within me. My reaction is a deep hurt; the playful remark is a more serious insult than was intended.

I react with a desire to *return the jab*. The right thing to do is ignore the remark or respond kindly and move on.

If I allow my ego to voice itself fully in reaction mode I may find myself ready to make an inappropriate remark that I will immediately regret.

All too often this is the case with reactions to workplace

comments.

Are You Listening Yet?

It's even easy to let the ego rule at home.

My wife, Paula, has used a phrase for many years. The comment sends waves of negative feelings through my entire body. I am ashamed to say that I have allowed myself to become angry at times. I have waited for an opportunity to direct the same comment toward her in an immature and vindictive manner.

"You're not listening!"

Sound familiar?

If I am not following what she is saying then the blame is on me. It's my fault for not comprehending the point she is making. I may not understand what she is saying because I am not fully engaged in the conversation or she may not be making herself clear to me. Either way, you know it is my fault! {Smile}

Regardless of whose fault it is, *"You're not listening"* feels like it is directed at my most vulnerable self.

One evening I'd heard that phrase for the thousandth time. I asked Paula if we could both create an intention to remove that decisive comment from our vocabulary.

I expressed to her that I perceived it as insulting; not at all conducive to constructive conversation.

I thought it would be more effective to use a replacement phrase such as, "I'm sorry. I must not be making myself clear." Or "I don't think you're getting my point."

These phrases seem less threatening.

Every time she stated, "You're not listening" there was an opportunity for me to make choices. I could ignore the comment and ask for clarification, acknowledge the fact that I may not have paid full attention and apologize or mention to her in a calm way that her comment was uncalled for and I was listening. Finally, ask her to please restate her point.

Our choices were directly affecting the outcome of our conversation, our feelings and emotions, our physical and mental states, and the direction of our relationship and our lives' path as well.

One simple choice between two people can create a relational landslide, or an opportunity to move in a mutually pleasing direction.

Is It Soup Yet?

What is the source of our choices? It's in the soup! That's right!

The soup contains the source of our choices. When our beliefs and intentions are the ingredients of the soup a lot of choices will emerge.

The combination of our beliefs and intentions determines the flavor of the soup, thus offering a wide array of choices.

If we want more choices, create more beliefs and intentions. The more choices we have, the more opportunities we create and the greater the chances for fulfillment.

The act of observing our choices may bring about additional choices. When we focus our attention on something, anything, it becomes more real to us. Our attention essentially solidifies reality. It brings the unknown into the realm of the known.

There may be choices that don't occur to us. We are inclined to make the first choice that comes to mind, the easiest choice, rather than the right choice. Other choices may be in the shadows waiting to come to the forefront. We want to cast light on every available choice so we can view the entire assemblage, then move forward allowing our heart to guide us with our feelings.

The first choice may not be the correct choice. At that moment though, the ego's choices may include reactions such as revenge, self-aggrandizement, subterfuge or recognition. This is where we should tame the ego by taking a breath and observing the choices.

When we direct our attention fully toward the situation at hand and perceive our feelings, we bring into focus not only the first choice, but the best choice or other alternatives.

Don't Drink the Water

Choices abound. Every second of every day we are bombarded with them.

The act of simply quenching our thirst is filled with choices. What should I drink? Should I buy a beverage or provide my own? Do I want a hot drink or a cold drink? A simple decision can become a fountain of choices.

We may not even notice the barrage of choices we make in a moment of time. Consider how many simple choices we make each day, consciously or unconsciously. The more we consider this the more we realize how many choices are available to us.

Humans overlook many daily opportunities to be aware of choices presenting themselves. We navigate our days on autopilot. We give little attention to the inconsequential decisions we are making.

With little attention to the choices we make sometimes the results and consequences of these actions can be devastating and debilitating. What control do you or I have over the outcomes of our choices?

The only control I have is over my own actions. I have little to do with the choices of others that affect me, although their choices may influence me. The best control I have over any situation is to make informed and smart choices based on the options presented to me.

When I feel positive about a choice; or see a positive outcome for me and others then I believe that I've made the best decision for me at this moment in time.

In contrast, if I feel uncomfortable, uneasy or sense that I may not have a positive outcome I should pause and review my choices.

One exercise I recommend is to visualize the possible outcomes of each situation. What do my instincts tell me?

Taking just a moment to allow our intuition to guide us brings forth more choices or an opportunity to review the options at hand.

Slowing down the conscious mind gives the heart a chance to open up and recognize what is best for us and those who surround us.

Chaotic Butterflies

Some choices result in benefits to ourselves, but can be a detriment to others. It may be impossible for us to fully realize the consequences of choices we are making and the affects they may have on other another individual. The chain of events that result from personal choices create implications to others in our world.

When a butterfly flaps its wings on one side of the world resulting in a series of events that unfolds into a hurricane on the other side of the world is known as *The Butterfly Effect,* or *Chaos Theory.* This would seem to be an extreme and random case of coincidence. However, the implications seem possible and relatable in other common situations.

Let's imagine that you have an older car that is in good operating condition. There is nothing wrong with it. You want to trade it in and purchase a different vehicle, or sell it yourself. You make the decision to sell your car privately, and buy another car.

You place a *For Sale* sign in the automobile's windshield. Your neighbor's car is broken. You are aware that he is facing financial hardship and his vehicle needs $2,000 in repairs. He needs a reliable vehicle, but only has $2,000 to his name.

He decides to purchase your used car for $2,000 rather than invest in repairs of his own. You sell your car to him for $2,000 and you are both satisfied with the transaction.

Two weeks later the car's transmission has a mechanical breakdown. Your neighbor receives the bad news; it will cost $4,000 to repair. He has no money left and does not have the ability to qualify for a loan.

He cannot pay for the needed repairs. He is unable to get to work and he loses his job. His life spirals out of control due to his financial hardships and layoff.

Neither of you knew that the car would break down. If you absolutely knew the scenario would play out this way perhaps out of concern for your neighbor you would have chosen to trade your car at an auto dealership.

Obviously your choices were not the only ones involved with your neighbor's dilemma. He had the free will to make an alternative choice. He might have shopped around for another car, or spent the $2,000 to get his car repaired.

Sometimes what appears to be a poor decision with a negative outcome may be a lesson that needs to be learned by all parties. Perhaps there is a higher meaning or practical wisdom to be gained through the process. We should be aware of the possible outcomes of the decisions we make. We should act in the best interest of ourselves and those around us.

Our lives should be an example of the maxim, "it is not always about me" and consider alternative choices.

As long as we remain open to the leading of our heart and make choices with integrity and honesty, we can't go wrong. Things may not always go our way but in the end we learn, we grow and we prosper spiritually, emotionally and, hopefully, financially as well.

Please take a moment to participate in the following exercise. It will expand your sense of purpose and allow your higher self to select the very best available choices that arise on your path to fulfillment.

Exercise Two

Awareness of Choice

Write the following questions on an index card or a sheet of paper. Review them each day, preferably in the morning, for a few days.

Read them each time a challenge or difficult choice appears in your life. After a few days of reviewing these questions you will automatically become more aware of your personal decision making style, especially if you create a belief about them and an intention to utilize the process to the fullest.

1. *Do I feel good in my heart about the choice I am making?*

2. *Is this choice in the best interest of myself and others that may be involved?*

3. *Is there an alternate choice that may be more beneficial to everyone involved?*

4. *What are the consequences that will be faced as result of this choice?*

Chapter Six

Actions Speak Louder Than Words

Action: 1) The process or state of acting or of being active. 2) Something done or performed; act; deed. 3) <u>An act that one consciously wills</u> and may be characterized by physical or mental activity. 4) Actions: habitual or usual acts; conduct. 5) Energetic activity. 6) An exertion of power or force. 7) Effect or influence.

- Webster's Unabridged Dictionary

"An act that one consciously wills" seems to sum it up. We may rely on our intuition to assist us with making choices but it is our action that moves us in the direction of our intentions via the will.

When we *will* something into being we have utilized deliberate action to bring about our intended result. It is at the very core of our existence that we find the makings of our *will*.

I recognize w*ill* as the power of control that the mind has over its own actions. Each of us possesses the power to control our actions through our will.

When we are determined and use our will to accomplish goals we are functioning as we were intended to. Our purpose for being is to create the life we desire for our self while serving the God of our heart.

Our will is our genie! "Your wish is my command" states the will. Our will has the power to choose our actions and follow through with them.

The actions we take lead us to the completion of our goals and intentions. When our actions are aligned with our intentions our lives are propelled forward to fulfillment. One can intend to become a master gardener but if he does not take action to study, learn and practice the ways of a master gardener he has little hope of becoming such.

A solid belief with strong intentions and good choices requires positive, steady *actions*. Actions are taken from the outset; beliefs depend on actions. Intentions require actions and choices must have action to move forward.

The Choice is Yours!

You've come to the realization that you are not listening very well to your spouse or friends when they are conversing with you. Your mind is wrapped up in mapping out your responses. You have only heard a small portion of what she is saying.

You want to change this behavior. You discover that you hold the belief, "What she is saying is not as important as what I'm thinking." You disregard this belief and create a new belief, "What others say is important. I always listen attentively."

This new belief must be followed up with a powerful intention to propel it forward. You create the intention, "Each time my friend talks to me I stop what I am doing or thinking and place my attention on her words and I become warmly connected with her."

This is what you intend to do from this moment forward. The Universe will now respond to you at each opportunity to serve your new intention.

The first opportunity to act on this intention arrives a few hours later. As you relax and read, your friend approaches you. She wants to share an experience from her workday.

If you are sincere about changing and your intention was powerful the first thing that should come to mind is your newly created intention.

At that very instant your choices will reveal themselves to you. First, do you stop reading and focus attention on your friend? Next, can you silence the chatter in your mind and listen attentively to your friend? Finally, will you continue to listen until she is finished?

These are just a few of the choices you'll be presented with as you focus on your new intention.

You will have choices that were not evident before you created the intention.

Choices are always present. They may be below the surface and out of your awareness but they are available at any time. The beauty of this process is that it opens the mind to additional possibilities.

You have created a new belief and new intention; new choices will now be brought to the forefront of your awareness. New outcomes are also invited into your world.

Action is what sets everything into forward motion. Your first action is to discover your hidden belief. Your next action is to create a new and positive belief. The action step following is the creation of a powerful intention and finally, your most important action is to make the very best choices guaranteeing the success of your intention.

Action does not stop there, and neither do subsequent

choices that arise along the journey to completion of your intention. If your intention is one that should be completed quickly in hours or days you still may have a multitude of choices available that will affect your outcome.

You may make choices that eventually bring about your desired intention, but may not have been the ideal choices. Other choices may have resulted in a much faster and more direct achievement of your goal.

Life allows us to 'begin again' at any point. Even if you make the wrong choice you may select another path. You may experience unpleasant obstacles along the way but you can discover new choices that bring you back to your original path.

Memories, like the corners of my mind....

It is difficult to make the right choices when we feel down, discouraged or ill. Our past may haunt us or our present be so stressful and difficult that we feel paralyzed with fear or doubt. Memories can trigger physiological changes that can be debilitating and must be addressed quickly and decisively.

When we remember terrible, frightening or shameful events we experience the emotional and sometimes physical pain and distress of the event as if it were occurring in real time.

The body locks away memories and when these recollections come to life again our body responds by reliving the experience. This recurrence of the experience can be as traumatic as the original event.

One may be haunted with the memory of a tragic accident involving a friend. Every time he sees his friend he recalls the accident that injured the friend and the guilt that accompanies it. The pain is real and may interfere with the person's decision making process.

When memories of past experiences are triggered individuals may be engulfed with emotion, reliving an event over and over resulting in a disconnection from the present. When we are in memory state reliving these negative events, we descend into a lower consciousness. Any state that disconnects us from the present moment is a lower level of consciousness.

"Nothing ever happened in the past that can prevent you from being present now; and if the past cannot prevent you from being present now, what power does it have?"
- Eckhart Tolle

The present moment is where life is, the past is where life was. The future is where life will be. We can do nothing about our past; it has already taken place.

We can do nothing about our future; it has not occurred. We have a direct impact on the present moment as this is where we exist right now.

The present is all that matters.

"Where you now stand is a direct result of thoughts and

feelings that you have offered before. Where you are going is a result of your perspective of where you now stand."

- Abraham-Hicks

What we do now will affect our future as our past is now affecting our present. Actions from our past affect our present, but only because we allow it. There is no past event or experience that can have any power over us until we give it power.

My father's suicide does not control my life or cause pain anymore. I made a choice not to let it have power over me. If I spent considerable time reliving that horrific day I would feel the pain, sorrow and guilt over again. I choose not to feel those emotions resulting from his action anymore.

I like feeling good! I like being happy! Happiness is a choice, as is feeling good, being at peace, feeling love, being grateful and living a fulfilled life.

Feeling miserable, unloved, guilty or unhappy are choices

as well. We can make deliberate choices to experience our life anyway we wish. No one forces us to act or feel the way we do. No one makes us feel bad or good, angry or happy. We control our attitude and emotions.

Sure, there are tough times, sadness, anger, fear or discouragement in life. However we may change those negative emotions into positive experiences and feelings at will. It is our will that determines how we choose to experience our world. When our will is strong we accomplish almost anything that our hearts desire.

We should recall traumatic or devastating events. We learn from these experiences. However we do not want to dwell on them, becoming a slave to them. Let them appear to you and then pass just like an automobile on the highway. Notice the recollection, and watch it go by and fade into the distance.

It's ok to remember wonderful, happy events too. Recalling pleasant experiences can engender a change in our emotional or physical state. Spend time remembering the good things in your past until your attitude shifts to a positive state. Then return to the present moment feeling more uplifted than before. Don't focus solely on your good feeling memories; that will create a false sense of reality.

Allow the warm feelings of good memories to carry over into your present state of being by using your will to bring you back into the now.

Use your will to bring you back into the present moment when painful memories resurface. If your present moment is too painful then focus your attention on a good memory, experience or happy time in your life until you begin to feel better.

Take a two minute break and complete the following exercise. This exercise is also found in Harry Palmer's book, *Resurfacing: Techniques for Exploring Consciousness,* from the Avatar materials.

It will give you a sense of how we may wield the power of will to change our state of being. When we are able to transition from one state of being into another with ease we will be in the driver's seat of our life.

Give it a try! The worst that can happen is you will muster up a smile and you just might brighten your day.

Exercise Three

The Will Rules All

Objective One: To reveal the effect that the will can have on a mental state via a deliberate physical action.

Instructions: Deliberately smile until you feel happy.

Yes, that's right; for a moment transform your face into a smiling face. Even if you are not happy at the moment, smile. If you don't feel like smiling or being happy, smile anyway and keep smiling.

Use your will to force the smile to continue for a moment longer and notice any changes you experience, mentally or emotionally.

Smile yourself into happiness!

Objective Two: *To show the effect that the will can have on physical action via a deliberate mental state.*

Instructions: *Think to yourself, "I am happy" until you smile.*

Maintain the thought that you are happy. Use your will to hold the thought steady in your mind. If you find yourself drifting away into other thoughts just bring yourself right back to "I am happy" and continue the exercise.

Envision a smile forming on your face as a result of your happy thoughts. Allow the transformation to begin.

Think yourself into a smile!

Did you smile yourself into happiness? Did you think yourself into happiness? Did you use your will to create a moment of happiness for yourself or were you preoccupied with unhappy thoughts?

If you were unable to smile, your will may need a tune up.

If you failed to create a smile I suggest running through this short exercise a few more times until a smile shines through.

Perhaps an easier way to utilize your will more effectively is to think of a time in your life when you experienced a joyous moment. Your extraordinary recollection might be the birth of your child, giving or receiving a gift that created incredible happiness, celebrating a birthday or promotion, a dream vacation, your first kiss, an accomplishment that you are proud of or a sacred moment of spirituality that was especially memorable.

Really look back on your life and choose something meaningful. Take your time. When you have locked on to it remember all of the details. Capture the feelings you experienced at the special moment. Experience all of the joy, wonder, elation, bliss, happiness, freedom, excitement, peacefulness or whatever good feelings settle in.

Enjoy the moment! Experience it fully and completely. Open your heart and mind, allow yourself to feel all the emotions as they arise. See the sights, hear the sounds, smell the scents, feel the physical and emotional sensations.

Pause for a moment and focus all of your attention on this process.

Continue reading when you have been successful at directing your will to bring about a pleasurable state. If your mind wanders refocus and bring your attention back to your memory. It's easier than you think once you find a meaningful, worthwhile memory that makes you feel good.

Do you feel, in the present, as you did when you experienced the event from the past?

Now remember a sad time in your life, tragic event, a death of a loved one, the loss of a job, an accident or illness, a failure, a broken relationship, that stands out in your mind.

Bring this memory to center stage and experience it completely.

Feel the pain, the sorrow, the agony, the sadness and despair, the loneliness or the emotion you experienced that is unpleasant and unsettling.

Completely experience the feelings and make it as real as possible. Experience all the sights, sounds and sensations associated with this tragic event. Take a moment to fully immerse yourself in the recollection.

Focus your attention on this memory. Bring forth the unpleasant feelings and sensations so they are similar to the original experience. Once you have accomplished this emotional state begin reading again. It may take a few moments for you to bring this into focus.

How was it possible to reconnect with the positive and uplifting memory and then so quickly experience the painful memory? How could you move from feeling warm and wonderful to sad or angry within just a moment?

You willed your attention to each memory, reached out and touched them one after the other. I imagine it was not very difficult to move between these recollections.

Revisit the happy memory once again to uplift yourself. Recall the good memories for a moment; or if you feel good just being in the present, enjoy that.

Hopefully you have experienced a major revelation. You changed your state from one extreme to another. It should have been quickly and easily performed.

Most people do not realize that we do this often; transitioning between memories and the present. We have the propensity to complete this exchange at will.

All we have to do is be aware of the opportunity to change from a negative to a positive state of mind. We can make the transition happen with the use of our will.

I hope you realize the importance of what you have accomplished. You have the means of enabling and empowering yourself to alter the course of your life at will.

Does the will rule all?

Are you ready to put it to work for you?

The present moment is where we want to function from. We may use the tools of the memory bank to bring ourselves into a more suitable state of being.

Anytime we are in a discouraged, depressed, angry or unhappy state we may think of a fond memory for a moment realizing that we can feel that way right now.

If you find yourself stuck in the painful past find a good memory to experience for a moment or bring yourself back into the present by focusing on the task at hand.

Consider what you are doing at the moment and place all of your attention on that, fully engaging in what you are presently doing. Your conscious mind will have less opportunity to wander into the past.

Experience the now instead of the past, but use your

shining, happy past experiences if you need a quick shift in your state.

It is your life to create as you will. If you need help from experiences use them. Decide how you wish to experience the moment you are in and use your will to keep you there.

"Sometimes your joy is the source of your smile, and sometimes your smile is the source of your joy."

> *Thich Nhat Hanh,*
> *Vietnamese Buddhist monk, teacher,*
> *author and peace activist*

Undivided We Stand, Divided We Fall

Gary was one of the best salespeople I ever worked with. He became one of my best managers. His fastidious attention to detail made him an excellent leader. He knew that he would get the most out of me if he had my complete attention.

Whenever he needed my advice or consultation he sat across from me, at my desk.

If I was working on something, giving only a portion of my attention to him, he announced to me, "Mr. Nelson, have I got your undivided attention?"

With this question he had my attention immediately.

The simple question made me realize that I was not giving him the attention he deserved.

I was multi-tasking; trying to be efficient with my very demanding schedule.

He was teaching me that we could accomplish more together if all attention was directed toward our mutually gratifying intentions with the business at hand.

When my attention was divided it was diluted and not as effective. When my attention was focused and controlled it was precise and powerful.

We accomplished more in a shorter period of time, with more effectiveness. There was nothing standing between us. There is great power invoked when two minds are synchronized and fully engaged without distractions.

Multitasking – Friend or Foe

I have always considered myself an excellent multitasker, handling the phone while working online with multiple windows open, creating reports, compiling research and more.

Recently, I was chatting online with a prospective client. During this interaction I received a phone call from another client.

As I juggled the two clients, retrieving requested information from different sources for each, I realized I was not fully present with either.

My responses to both were slowing. I sensed that one or both clients were aware that I was handling other issues, while trying to focus on them. I sensed that they knew I was not giving either of them the attention they deserved.

The person I was chatting with online left the conversation before I was able to furnish all their requested information. I had no contact information for them and was unable to make amends for my lack of attention. At least by ending the chat I was able to fully direct my attention to the client on the phone.

This was a difficult, but important lesson, for me to learn. There are pitfalls to multitasking. There are times when multitasking is not only inappropriate but ineffective.

Recent studies at Stanford University suggest that "heavy media multitaskers are poor at multitasking and at a number of cognitive processes." (www.stanford.edu/~nass/)

Evidently we multitasking junkies get our fix by the multimedia input. We rarely possess the ability to perform the multitasking effectively.

This was a total surprise to me. I felt I was proficient with my multitasking skills; although, I became overwhelmed at times with the quantity of information on my plate.

I would then succumb to narrowing my activities down to the most important at hand, working toward efficiently completing those on a one by one basis.

Roll over Beethoven!

I was in an automobile accident over a decade ago. As I was turning off the main road I was hit from behind by two cars in a domino effect. Both drivers were traveling in excess of 55 mph when they struck me, one after the other.

The impact caused my vehicle to roll multiple times. My driver's seat broke from the hinges upon impact.

I suffered a severe concussion in addition to other injuries.

One long-lasting and chronic condition resulting from this accident was Tinnitus, with symptoms including a loud and constant ringing in my ears.

The disorder is extremely distracting. It occasionally swells to a high pitched noise that fills my head with sounds and pressures that stops me in my tracks. The sensation and sounds are chronic, always present in varying degrees of pitch and volume.

If I focus my attention on the sounds for an instant they become magnified and are brought to the forefront of my conscious state. I literally turn up the volume myself.

To relieve the symptoms and reduce the effects I focus my

attention on the task at hand. Once my attention shifts to an object or situation the sounds diminish to a lower lever which I filter out more easily.

Anything we focus our attention on becomes more real and apparent to us. As our objects of desire come to the forefront the objects we wish to avoid fade into the background.

We control our feelings through personal choice.

When an angry moment besets us we choose to let it go and transition into feeling good. If we are unhappy we can pretend, remember or smile ourselves back into a happy state. The mind recognizes our body language. We can fool the mind into happiness by smiling our way through unhappy events.

This transition may be difficult to pull off when in an undesirable state. In the grips of anger or frustration the last thing we want to do is smile!

If we remove ourselves from the emotional attachment to the unpleasant event using our will we might break out of that condition.

The picture of my family I keep in my office helps me do that on many occasions. Just one look and I feel that warm, loving tingle vibrate through my being.

This is one method of changing our state of mind. It is quite alright to experience anger, frustration or other negative emotions that we create. It is not healthy to remain in a negative state too long. Once we find ourselves in this emotional state we can decide to change it quickly and move on.

You Can't Make Me Do It!

No one can *make* us angry or sad. This is not something another individual has control over.

We are the only one who can make us angry or sad.

It is a choice we make and it is totally our decision. Circumstances can invite us into these states but you must either accept the invitation and act upon it or ignore the inducement and choose to be free from it. With practice the decision becomes easier and easier. Creating the state we feel most comfortable in is our choice.

It's like removing the bacon from a hot pan on a stove. It stops cooking instantly!

Remove yourself from the environment, physically or mentally, and you will cease to cook.

Think about how you would prefer to feel. Make it your complete intention to alter your state.

I'm sure you have heard of the ten-two letter words: "If it is to be it is up to me!"

It is totally up to me. I hold the responsibility for how I want to feel. Nobody can make that choice for me.

My favorite mantra is, "I am as I decide to be!" I have this posted in my office and reflect on it often.

I decide to be happy.

I decide to be at peace.

I decide exactly how I wish to experience life.

I am as I decide to be!

Chapter Seven

Tying it All Together and Making it Happen

I am not immune to negative states of being. I experience a range of emotions in my day to day life.

I get angry, discouraged, sad, hurt, frustrated and just plain pissed off at times.

Just ask my wife!

The intention of this book is not to bring perfection in your life. The words and ideas are meant to provide a means of support and direction to a more fulfilling life. All it takes is a few minor tweaks in thought and behavior to bring about massive change.

I have experienced extraordinary change and it is an ongoing improvement in my daily life.

Life has never been better or more enjoyable.

I was prone to daily frustration prior to mastering these methods. I now experience frustration only occasionally. Instead of unhappiness with my circumstances, I am rarely unhappy.

I experienced overwhelming stress daily. Now I focus my thoughts on my powerful intentions; constantly bringing myself into the present moment where I attract the feelings and emotions I desire.

Just Let It Go!

Early in my marriage I found myself angry for days after an argument with my wife. I held on to anger and hurt and kept them close to my heart and mind.

Paula would often ask me why I continued to be angry at her. She wondered why I could not let my anger go. I wondered the same.

After 33 years of marriage we still have occasional arguments but now each of us puts the situation behind us quickly.

If you want to improve the quality of your life and experience positive change, make your commitment to follow the methods outlined in this book.

If you were a golfer and I knew a method to improve your game in a small amount of time, wouldn't you invest the time to practice a few simple exercises?

This is *your* game of life we are taking about. This process will improve the way you experience your life. It will enhance your ability to adapt to changes, obtain your goals, drastically reduce procrastination and adjust to life's ever changing flow.

Here is a short list of suggestions for using this book to make quick improvements on your quest for living a more fulfilled life.

1. Begin slowly. Pick one or two things you want to change or improve in the first week. There will be plenty of time during the rest of your life for as many changes as you wish.

2. If one of the exercises does not have an impact, move to the next. Don't worry about whether it worked. You can always come back to it in the future.

3. Take time to consider what areas of your life you want to improve. Procrastination, relationships, business or personal goals, your physical, mental or emotional health, past experiences, attitudes. Make note of them so you can focus on them when the time is appropriate.

4. Have fun with the process! Proceed with the wonder of a child and the excitement of an explorer. Allow it to unfold as it will. Do not force

outcomes. The process will work once you put it into action.

Examples of my Personal Intentions

Here is a sampling of my personal beliefs and intentions that I have successfully used in the past and present. I carry a miniaturized list in my wallet and review them when I feel a need for a reminder, (which is pretty darn often). I had transparent beliefs but I have discarded them as they were of no use to me.

I find it extremely useful to integrate the feeling that the beliefs arouse into my written intentions. This is how I feel while experiencing my intended desires. I incorporate these words into my intentions. That feeling is a powerful catalyst in creating a reality from an intention. That feeling is an end result of a worthwhile intention.

Beliefs	Intentions
It's ok to make mistakes. Mistakes are learning tools.	*I feel good easily avoiding frustration while making mistakes.*
Mistakes are acceptable.	*I learn good lessons from my mistakes and they are rewarding experiences.*

In the past I felt horrible when I made mistakes. This is now a learning experience. I feel empowered when I make mistakes. That allows opportunity to turn those mistakes into positive gains.

Beliefs	Intentions
My level of patience has nothing to do with my age.	*I amaze myself at how well I utilize patience daily to improve my state of being.*
I have more patience than I am aware of.	*I feel sensational when I experience patience.*
I am patient with myself and others.	*I feel great when I am patient with everyone.*

The disabling feeling of impatience has morphed into a satisfying sense of being during the times I utilize this intention.

Belief	Intention
I have time to help others.	*Going out of my way to help others in life is essential and feels right.*

This is one of my most satisfying intentions. There are so many daily opportunities to help others. It feels great going beyond the call of duty to assist others, even in the smallest ways.

I am reminded of one of Dr. Deepak Chopra's mantras, "How may I serve?" Service to others lies at the heart of humanity and it soothes my being and provides a greater sense of connection to all that is.

Belief	Intention
What others think of me has no meaning.	*It makes me happy bringing reusable shopping bags to the grocery store.*

For years I tried to remember to bring reusable bags to the grocery store. I constantly forgot them. I would give up and leave them at home out of frustration. Finally, I realized that I could create a powerful intention that would eliminate the fear of what others were thinking about me. A few years ago it was uncommon to see male shoppers bring their own bags to the grocer. I felt I stuck out among the shoppers who didn't bother with their own bags. My powerful intention eliminated the fear of what shoppers and employees thought of me for bringing my own bags into the store.

It was the right thing to do and I now shop free of

worries of what others think. It's commonplace for shoppers to bring their own bags now. In the early days of this positive trend my powerful intention provided a way for me to participate without the worries of feeling like an odd standout.

Belief	Intention
I foster relationships based on love and concern.	*I feel fantastic being proactive with calls, cards and emails on a regular basis with my friends and relatives.*

This powerful intention is an ongoing process. Communicating regularly with my family and friends is more difficult than I imagined. However, I am gaining ground and it feels satisfying.

Belief	Intention
I am interested in what Paula has to say.	*I listen to Paula carefully and attentively and it makes both of us feel warm and wonderful.*

Listening to Paula with openness and interest is another ongoing project. I am constantly reminded of my intention to slow down and listen, really listen, to what she is saying. The intention is making a difference. I am happy with my progress. Our communication levels are more real than they have been in a long time.

Belief	Intention
I have plenty of time to meditate each day.	*My daily meditation practice improves my physical, mental and spiritual being. I feel great as a result.*

As each day passes the importance of my meditation practice becomes more evident. Time I set aside to be silent, reflective and introspective sets the pace for my day. I feel much better when I meditate, even for ten to fifteen minutes. The rewards are great.

Belief	Intention
I am the silent observer.	*Each day I notice my ego reacting to situations. When I choose to respond with love I feel connected.*

I am not happy or content when my ego rules my world. It needs to be tamed moment by moment. When I control my ego and observe my reactions the results are positive, meaningful and significant. Constantly existing in this space would be total bliss.

Belief	Intention
I enjoy my good health. Feeling healthy results in personal happiness.	*When I consciously eat healthy foods I feel vibrant and healthy. If I indulge in foods that I love in moderation I feel satisfied.*

Dark chocolate and savory cheese crackers are vices of mine. If left unchecked I would easily devour a box of crackers and excessive amounts of dark chocolate. It takes a strong will and consistent effort to manage cravings with my intentions.

I review my intentions often. I feel gratitude when I am able to withstand the temptations. My powerful intentions are there to protect me from my indiscretions. I use them to my advantage.

You may wonder how one is able to keep up with so many beliefs and intentions. This is a partial list that I have developed for myself. Sometimes one gets lost in the shuffle. To organize myself I keep a current list of my beliefs and intentions in my pocket, in my office and on my intention board at home. I can easily review when necessary.

Remove your completed intentions from your list. Upon completion the former intention goes off the list as my completed garden did.

Ongoing intentions should remain on your list until they are solidified and fully embraced.

In closing....

I enjoy life more than ever. I am attaining goals, adapting to change, growing and realizing my potential. It feels incredibly wonderful and liberating.

I thrive within a system that monitors my actions and guides me in staying on track with my goals and intentions.

If you feel this system will guide you in the right direction, help keep you focused on your personal and business success I encourage you to place your trust in this process. Allow it to work for you.

If this book helps you improve one area of your life or one issue that you would like to handle then I am happy and you should be too.

Experience has taught me that this process will guide you in many areas of your life.

Every time you have a victory, even a small victory, a new sense of happiness and fulfillment will arise within you. It will inspire you to attempt another victory.

A series of small victories culminates into a big win.

It is easy to experience a small victory. Any win feels good and with each new victory your enthusiasm for the next will grow.

As you celebrate these accomplishments your attitude will change and your sense of being the creator of your life will expand. You'll understand that life does not have to be lived in leaps and bounds, but can be enjoyed one small step at a time.

Sometimes lives become stagnant. People are waiting for the big play and only want to move forward if it is a giant step. Striving for the giant steps in life could result in missed opportunities to make small gains.

Smaller gains may seem inconsequential but moving toward stated goals and intentions is positive advancement in your life.

"None of us know what the next change is going to be, what unexpected opportunity is just around the corner, waiting a few months or a few years to change all the tenor of our lives."

I love this quote by Kathleen Norris. One of those small steps or small victories could invoke a change that leads to the biggest opportunity of your life. Remember the Butterfly Effect?

I'll conclude with one final quote by the American astronaut, Neil Armstrong. Armstrong was stepping onto the moon when he uttered the famous words, "That's one small step for [a] man, one giant leap for mankind."

I invite you to take that one small step in the area of your life that you desire improvement. Consider the possibility of improvement in all phases of your life with each step, no matter how small or large it may be.

One small victory can evolve into many great victories.

A victorious life is an enriched and fulfilled life. This life is available to you at any moment.

Banish the doubt, move into solid beliefs, powerful intentions and mindful, deliberate choices.

About The Author

After witnessing his father's suicide at the impressionable age of fifteen, the author experienced many years of guilt, shame, and fear with countless thoughts of suicide which finally resulted in the manifestation of physical disease.

Living in a miserable emotional and physical state for so long led him to seek out ways of discovering the means to liberate himself from his haunting past and the ensuing physical deterioration.

Research in various fields of study including spiritual paths and ontology, science and medicine, psychology and health became his undertaking for more than twenty years.

He read many books, immersed himself in volumes of audio and video programs, attended numerous seminars amounting to well over 400 hours of experiential classroom practice.

The culmination of this lengthy, yet worthwhile, journey yielded the discovery of quick and easy means of eliminating procrastination and destructive behavioral patterns while creating a sense of self-empowerment and fulfillment.

The author experienced an awakening in the middle of the night, being greeted by a voice calling him to share with others the techniques he had learned. The time to share this invaluable information is now!

This leading of his heart and spirit was to remind him to give back to the world the love and knowledge given to him while on his path. This book is for those who are ready to make the change from suffering or struggling with life to allowing empowerment to pervade their lives.

The author's powerful intention is to teach others to create happiness and bliss in their lives. "Life shouldn't be a struggle" says the author, "So many people are striving to experience just a measure happiness and fulfillment in their lives. Happiness, joy, fulfillment, success and peace should be abundant in our lives. This book will provide answers for those who just can't seem to find their way through the fog."

Visit my website at **AwakenMyPotential.com** for more information, my blog and upcoming books.

You will find my second book, **The Mindfulness Approach: To Eliminate or Reduce Symptoms of Stress-Related Illnesses**, on my website or on Amazon.com and Kindle.

Recommended Resources

AvatarEPC.com is a great place to visit. There are several mini-courses you can download for free or you can purchase the book, "The Seven Pillars of Enlightenment" for the complete set: http://www.avatarbookstore.com/component/content/article/9-seven-pillars-of-enlightenment.html.
Also available are DVD's, other books and more information about how to get your life freed up so you can begin to live deliberately in the moment and create the life of your dreams.

You may contact Avatar at:

Star's Edge International

237 North Westmonte Drive

Altamonte Springs, FL 32714

(407) 788-3090

avatar@avatarhq.com

Avatar® and Star's Edge International® are registered trademarks of Star's Edge, Inc

All rights reserved.

www.ingramcontent.com/pod-product-compliance
Lightning Source LLC
Chambersburg PA
CBHW060153050426
42446CB00013B/2810